NARENDRA MODI

The Man Behind The Vision

Dr. Rajeev Madhavan Menon

PG PUBLICATION

Delhi 110089 (India)

Edition : 2024
ISBN : 978-81-969762-5-5

Price : 600/-

NARENDRA MODI-THE MAN BEHIND THE VISION
Dr. Rajeev Madhavan Menon

Cover page & Layout
Jyoti Singh

Published by

PRAKHAR GOONJ PUBLICATION
Reg. Office: H-3/2 Sector-18 Rohini, Delhi-110089
Office : A-4/57 Sector-18 Rohini, Delhi-110089
Email : prakhargoonj@gmail.com
info@prakhargoonjpublications.com
Ph. :7982710571, 7838505899, 011-42635077
Web : prakhargoonjpublications.com

NARENDRA MODI
The Man Behind The Vision

CONTENTS

Chapter 1

Narendra Modi's Early Life, Education, and Influences

Narendra Modi was born on September 17, 1950, in Vadnagar, a small town in the western Indian state of Gujarat. His early life was marked by modest circumstances. His family belonged to the Ghanchi community, which traditionally worked with oil and belonged to the Other Backward Classes (OBC) category. Modi's childhood was spent in a simple environment, and he helped his father sell tea at Vadnagar Railway Station during his early years.

He pursued his education at local schools in Vadnagar and later moved to Ahmedabad, the largest city in Gujarat, for higher studies. There, he completed a Bachelor's degree in Political Science from the University of Delhi. Despite not excelling academically, his time in Delhi sparked an interest in politics and the Rashtriya Swayamsevak Sangh (RSS), a Hindu nationalist organization.

Political Journey:

Narendra Modi's political journey is marked by several significant milestones:

1. **Early RSS Involvement:** Modi joined the RSS as a pracharak (campaigner) in his early years. This association laid the foundation for his political and ideological development. The RSS, known for its Hindutva ideology, played a pivotal role in shaping his beliefs.

2. **Chief Minister of Gujarat**: In 2001, Modi was appointed as the Chief Minister of Gujarat, one of India's most economically dynamic states. During his tenure, Gujarat experienced rapid economic

growth, earning him a reputation as a pro-business and development-oriented leader. However, his time as Chief Minister was also marred by controversy due to the handling of the 2002 Gujarat riots, which resulted in significant communal violence and loss of life.

3. **Rise Within the BJP:** Modi's political acumen and charisma led to his ascent within the Bharatiya Janata Party (BJP), the political wing of the RSS. He gained prominence for his economic policies and administrative skills.

4. **2014 General Elections:** In 2014, Narendra Modi led the BJP to a historic victory in the Indian general elections. He was sworn in as the Prime Minister of India. His campaign focused on promises of economic growth and development, often citing the "Gujarat model" as an example of his vision.

5. **Reelection in 2019:** Modi was reelected as Prime Minister in the 2019 general elections, securing a significant majority in the Lok Sabha. His leadership continued with a renewed mandate.

Key Context:

Understanding Narendra Modi's leadership requires an appreciation of the broader political and social context:

1. **Hindutva and Nationalism:** Modi's political ideology is deeply rooted in Hindutva, which emphasizes the cultural and religious identity of Hindus. His government often championed nationalism, emphasizing pride in India and its traditions.

2. **Economic Reforms:** Modi's tenure saw the introduction of transformative economic reforms,

such as the Goods and Services Tax (GST) and initiatives like "Make in India" aimed at boosting manufacturing and business growth.

3. **Foreign Policy**: Modi pursued an active foreign policy, strengthening ties with key nations like the United States and seeking to enhance India's global standing.

4. **Controversies and Criticisms:** Modi's leadership faced criticism and controversy on various fronts, including concerns about religious and social issues, handling of dissent, and debates over freedom of expression.

5. **COVID-19 Pandemic:** During his second term, Modi faced the immense challenge of managing the COVID-19 pandemic in India, drawing international attention due to the country's large population and healthcare infrastructure constraints.

Narendra Modi's background, marked by humble beginnings, and his political journey, from being a pracharak in the RSS to becoming India's Prime Minister, reflect a remarkable ascent in Indian politics. Understanding the broader context of his leadership is essential to comprehending his impact on India's political landscape, economic reforms, foreign policy, and the controversies that have surrounded his tenure. Public perceptions of Modi's leadership remain diverse, making his legacy a subject of continued debate and analysis.

The purpose of the biography

The purpose of this detailed biography on Narendra Modi, the 14th Prime Minister of India, is to offer readers a comprehensive and nuanced exploration of his life, his ascent in Indian politics, his policies, and his impact on the nation. This biography aims to provide an in-depth understanding of Narendra Modi as both a political figure and a person.

1. **Unveiling the Man Behind the Leader:** This biography aims to uncover the layers of Narendra Modi's persona, starting with his early life, upbringing, and personal experiences. By delving into his formative years, readers can grasp the influences that have shaped his character, ideology, and values.

2. **The Political Odyssey:** A central objective of this biography is to trace Narendra Modi's remarkable political journey. It begins with his humble origins as a Rashtriya Swayamsevak Sangh (RSS) pracharak and charts his meteoric rise within the Bharatiya Janata Party (BJP). The narrative navigates through the twists and turns of his career, culminating in his elevation to the position of Prime Minister.

3. **Governance and Policy Reforms:** A significant portion of this biography is dedicated to Modi's tenure as Prime Minister. It provides a detailed analysis of his approach to governance, highlighting his signature initiatives such as "Make in India," "Swachh Bharat Abhiyan" (Clean India Mission), and the bold but controversial demonetization move. By examining these policies, readers gain insight into Modi's vision for India's development.

4. **Impact on India and the World:** This biography explores the profound impact of Narendra Modi's leadership on India, both domestically and on the global stage. It delves into his foreign policy decisions, including the "Act East" policy, and examines his handling of India's complex relations with Pakistan and China. Readers gain an appreciation of how Modi's leadership has shaped India's standing in the world.

5. **Controversies and Criticisms:** To present a balanced narrative, this biography does not shy away from addressing controversies and criticisms associated with Narendra Modi. It delves into contentious issues like the Gujarat riots of 2002, the debate surrounding his leadership style, and allegations of intolerance during his tenure.

6. **An Inspirational Journey:** Through the detailed recounting of Narendra Modi's life story, this biography aims to inspire and motivate readers. It underscores how an individual from modest beginnings can rise to one of the world's most influential positions through unwavering determination and relentless effort.

7. **Historical Record:** Beyond serving as a source of inspiration, this biography contributes to the historical record. It meticulously documents the events, decisions, and milestones of Narendra Modi's life and career, serving as a valuable resource for future generations to study and analyse.

In conclusion, the purpose of this detailed biography on Narendra Modi is to provide readers with a comprehensive and intricate exploration of his life and political journey. It strives to be a source of knowledge, inspiration, and insight into the leadership of one of India's most prominent figures. Whether readers admire or critique him, understanding Narendra Modi's life and impact is essential to comprehending contemporary Indian politics and history.

1. **Birth and Family:** Narendra Modi was born on September 17, 1950, in Vadnagar, a small town in Gujarat, India. His family was not wealthy. His father, Damodardas Modi, had a small tea stall at the Vadnagar Railway Station. His mother's name was

Hiraben. Modi had five siblings, and he was the third child. They lived a modest life.

2. **Childhood Years:** During Modi's childhood, he was very curious and had a strong desire to learn new things. He attended the local school in Vadnagar. Teachers described him as a diligent student who worked hard and occasionally participated in debates and drama.

3. **Interest in the RSS:** As a teenager, Modi developed an interest in the RSS, a group with specific ideas about India's identity. This marked his initial foray into politics and his contemplation of the country's future.

4. **Marriage and Early Life:** Modi's family arranged his marriage to Jashodaben when he was still very young. However, their marriage did not work out, and they lived separately. Modi made the decision to dedicate his life to public service and left his family to explore different parts of India.

5. **Entry into Politics:** Modi embarked on his political journey in the 1970s when he joined a political party called the BJP. He demonstrated exceptional organizational skills and unwavering dedication to the party's principles.

6. **Becoming Chief Minister:** Modi's hard work paid off, and he served as the Chief Minister of Gujarat, a state in India, for four terms. His leadership was well-received by the people.

7. **Becoming Prime Minister:** In 2014, Narendra Modi led the BJP to a significant victory in India's general elections, propelling him to the position of Prime Minister of India, the leader of the entire country.

Narendra Modi's life story exemplifies that with determination and effort, anyone can achieve great things, regardless of their starting point. His journey from a humble family in Vadnagar to becoming the Prime Minister of India serves as an inspiration to many.

8. **Family Background:** Narendra Modi was born into a humble family in Vadnagar, Gujarat, India. His father, Damodardas Modi, ran a small tea stall at the Vadnagar Railway Station, while his mother, Hiraben, took care of their home. Modi had five siblings, and he was the third child. Their family had limited financial resources, and they led a modest life.

9. **Upbringing:** Modi's childhood was characterized by simplicity and hard work. He attended the local school in Vadnagar and was known as a curious and eager student. Even at a young age, he displayed leadership qualities and occasionally participated in debates and drama at school.

Early Life Challenges

1. **Interest in RSS (Rashtriya Swayamsevak Sangh):** As a teenager, Modi developed an interest in the RSS, a group with specific ideas about India's identity and culture. The RSS emphasized physical fitness, character-building, and social service. Modi found their ideology, and he became an RSS pracharak, actively working to spread their ideas.

   Modi's involvement with the RSS played a crucial role in his early life, introducing him to the world of politics and shaping his thinking and beliefs. This foundation would later pave the way for his significant political journey in India.

2. **Schooling:** Narendra Modi's early schooling occurred in Vadnagar, a small town in Gujarat, India. He attended the local school where his thirst for knowledge became evident from a young age. Narendra was a diligent and inquisitive student. His teachers described him as disciplined and responsible. Even as a child, he showed leadership qualities by participating in activities like debates and drama.

3. **College Years:** Upon completing his school education, Narendra Modi pursued higher studies at the University of Delhi located in India's capital, New Delhi. At college, he chose to study political science, a subject that would later become pivotal in his life. College was a new and exciting experience for him, but he remained dedicated to his studies. During these years, Modi's interest in politics started to take root. This burgeoning fascination with politics laid the foundation for his future involvement in Indian politics.

Narendra Modi's schooling and college years were characterized by his dedication to learning and an emerging passion for politics. These formative years played a crucial role in shaping him into the prominent leader he would become in India.

Narendra Modi, the 14th Prime Minister of India, was shaped by various key influences during his early life. These influences helped mold his character and played a significant role in his political journey. Let's delve into these influences in detail, using straightforward language.

1. **Humble Upbringing:** Modi was born on September 17, 1950, in Vadnagar, a small town in Gujarat, India. His family belonged to the Ghanchi community, which was considered socially and economically underprivileged. Growing up in a modest environment

taught him the values of simplicity, hard work, and frugality.

2. **Early Struggles:** His family faced financial difficulties, and Modi had to help his father run a tea stall at the Vadnagar railway station during his teenage years. This experience instilled in him a strong work ethic and a deep understanding of the struggles faced by ordinary people.

3. **Influence of RSS:** In his early teens, Modi became associated with the Rashtriya Swayamsevak Sangh (RSS), a right-wing Hindu nationalist organization. The RSS provided him with a sense of purpose and a platform for grassroots work. He learned organizational skills and developed a keen interest in politics and social issues.

4. **Association with Akhil Bharatiya Vidyarthi Parishad (ABVP):** While studying at Delhi University, Modi became an active member of the ABVP, the student wing of the RSS. This marked his entry into student politics, where he honed his leadership skills and gained exposure to a broader range of political ideologies.

5. **Mentorship of L.K. Advani:** Modi's association with senior BJP leader L.K. Advani was pivotal in his political career. Advani recognized Modi's potential and mentored him, giving him opportunities within the Bharatiya Janata Party (BJP). This association played a crucial role in Modi's rise within the party ranks.

6. **Chief Minister of Gujarat:** Modi's tenure as the Chief Minister of Gujarat from 2001 to 2014 was a significant turning point. His leadership during the aftermath of the 2002 Gujarat riots garnered both

praise and criticism. Nevertheless, it solidified his position as a strong and decisive leader.

7. **Economic Reforms in Gujarat:** As Chief Minister, Modi focused on economic development, attracting investments, and infrastructure improvement. His policies in Gujarat were seen as business-friendly, which later became a central theme of his national governance.

8. **Influence of Swami Vivekananda:** Modi often cites Swami Vivekananda as a major influence on his life. He admires Vivekananda's teachings on spirituality, nationalism, and the importance of youth in nation-building.

9. **Digital Savvy:** Modi embraced technology and social media early in his political career. He recognized the power of digital communication in reaching a vast audience and used it effectively during his campaigns, particularly in the 2014 and 2019 general elections.

I Narendra Modi's early key influences were rooted in his humble beginnings, his association with the RSS and ABVP, mentorship by leaders like L.K. Advani, and his experiences as the Chief Minister of Gujarat. These experiences shaped him into the influential political leader he is today, with a focus on economic development, nationalism, and the use of technology in governance.

CHAPTER 2

Early Life In Brief And The Cultural Influences on Narendra Modi's Path to Leadership.

Narendra Modi's birthplace is Vadnagar, a small town in Gujarat, located approximately 110 kilometers directly north of his current residence, the chief minister's bungalow in Gandhinagar. While geographically close, symbolically, it represents a significant journey from his humble beginnings.

India's inaugural general election occurred shortly following the birth of Narendra Modi. The Indian National Congress, led by Pandit Jawaharlal Nehru, secured a resounding victory by capturing 364 out of the then 489 seats in the Lok Sabha. Subsequently, after the tumultuous period of Independence and Partition, the democratically elected Union government commenced its operations in accordance with the Indian Constitution, which was officially enacted on January 26, 1950. As Prime Minister Nehru addressed the nation in 1952, a young Narendra Modi, much to the delight of his parents, was in the process of developing his earliest vocabulary.

In the year 1950, Vadnagar exuded a serene, semi-rural charm, though somewhat weathered and devoid of access to electricity. The inhabitants of this town harbored modest ambitions, often mirroring the socio-economic status of their parents. During this era, India was not a nation known for its burgeoning social mobility or abundant opportunities, and for the majority, life followed a predictable, self-contained routine.

One could draw a parallel between Vadnagar and the larger context of India, as both seemed to have a rich historical past that lay mostly in ruins. To the north of the town, majestic remnants provided glimpses of an ancient epicenter, bearing testimony to its erstwhile role as a grand and commanding regional capital, stretching back millennia.

When reflecting on his childhood, Modi often alludes to a bygone era in Vadnagar's history, one where this town once housed a thriving community of 10,000 Buddhist monks. Undoubtedly, the archaeological wealth of the region attests to a fascinating and influential past, although this epoch has receded into the distant annals of history.

However, by the year 1950, the Indian populace, including the residents of Narendra Modi's hometown, had undergone a series of transformations wrought by waves of invasions and colonial rule spanning centuries. These experiences had compelled them to recalibrate their aspirations to more modest levels. Nevertheless, a glimmer of optimism had begun to emerge as they cautiously began to envision a future they could shape for themselves. This vision, while distant and undefined, offered a slender but palpable thread of hope for something better on the horizon.

The railway had long been a fixture in Vadnagar, and in this backdrop, Damodardas, the father of Narendra Modi, made his livelihood by operating a modest tea stall situated on the town's railway station platform. This small establishment, which endures to this day, retains its weathered character – a humble shed constructed from blue-grey tin or steel, adorned with patches, and bearing the marks of time. Its antiquity mirrors the architectural style of the platform it occupies, sheltered beneath its eaves.

Damodardas hailed from a family named Ranchoddas, who relocated to Vadnagar in the late nineteenth century with the aim of establishing a grocery store. In 1950, he was thirty-five years old and married to Hiraben, a native of the town. At the time of Narendra's birth, he joined two older siblings, Som, then six years old, and Amrit, just four. Subsequently, the family expanded to include a sister, Vasanti, born two years after Narendra, followed by two more brothers, Prahlad in 1955, and Pankaj in 1958.

The Modi family's financial circumstances, measured by contemporary standards, were decidedly modest. However, within the context of their era and the local community, they did not perceive themselves as markedly disadvantaged. Their involvement in the tea business, though modest, elevated them beyond the uncertain livelihoods typical of day labourers or sharecroppers during that period.

The Modi family, consisting of both parents, siblings, and sister, resided in a modest three-room dwelling constructed from a combination of brick and mud. This single-story abode, while not exceptionally small, measured approximately 40 feet by 12 feet in dimensions. The front section comprised a bedroom and a sitting room, overlooking an unpaved lane, while the central area housed a dimly lit kitchen. Towards the rear, there was a storage room for fuel. The household's water supply necessitated fetching from a nearby well, and storage relied on clay vessels. The flooring consisted of bamboo covered with mud, and notably, the absence of windows in the walls meant that when the cooking fire, fueled by cow dung, was ignited, the air within would become thick and smoky.

In the social context, the Modis, belonging to the Muslim Ghanchis community in Gujarat, fell within the category of OBC (Other Backward Caste). It's worth clarifying that OBC status does not necessarily equate to being of low caste. The Modis, as part of the Ghanchis, occupied a position within the broader spectrum of labourers and could be described as lower-middle-class individuals, albeit with numerous Indian castes beneath them.

The extent to which young Narendra would have been affected by his social rank and any associated disadvantages in the small rural town of his upbringing remains uncertain.

It is likely that during his formative years, he may have been relatively unaware of these factors. Remarkably, this social positioning seemed to have left no discernible imprint on his sense of identity, devoid of sentiments such as resentment or inferiority. Even in the realm of political discourse, he rarely invokes his origins to substantiate his arguments, even though it could potentially bolster his position.

The Modi family resided in a closely-knit neighborhood, situated near Vadnagar's Muslim community. Interactions with Muslim neighbors were commonplace, and a significant portion of Narendra's childhood friends were of the Muslim faith. One of his closest companions was Jasood Khan Pathan. He participated in both Muslim and Hindu religious festivals without a sense of peculiarity, and this harmonious coexistence went unremarked upon by his family or the parents of his playmates. Narendra was affectionately referred to as 'ND,' derived from his paternal initials, "Damodardas."

Numerous anecdotes exist that shed light on Narendra's demeanor during his school years. He displayed a strong work ethic in the classroom and exhibited an early aptitude for rhetoric as a member of the school's debating society. One frequently recounted incident underscores his unwavering determination when he adamantly insisted that only the teacher should evaluate his homework, refusing to allow a class monitor to do so. However, initial impressions can sometimes be misleading, as many accomplished school debaters pursue careers in fields like banking or retail management, and academically exceptional students may later find themselves in roles as office managers or mid-level bureaucrats.

Childhood tales often provide pre-packaged narratives that seamlessly fit into the mosaic portrait of a leader. Occasionally, these stories acquire a legendary quality. For instance, it is well-documented that Narendra enjoyed swimming in the nearby Sharmishtha Lake, an activity that carried a certain element of risk due to the presence of crocodiles in the waters. An early narrative involving Narendra and the lake tells of an ancient shrine, or in later versions, a beautiful temple, perched on a rocky outcrop not far from the lake's shore.

During certain significant religious observances, the need arose to replace the small flag adorning a particular shrine. On one such occasion, following a heavy rain that had stirred the crocodile inhabitants, there was a requirement to change the flag. Despite receiving counsel against it, Narendra, accompanied by two companions, Mahendra and Bachu, undertook the perilous swim to the outcrop and back. In later years, this outcrop would transform into a distant island, and Narendra would swim this route alone. Meanwhile, onlookers on the shoreline employed the rhythmic beating of drums, presumably to deter the reptiles or divert them from the path of the young swimmers.

Narendra successfully accomplished the flag replacement and was met with resounding cheers from the now significantly augmented crowd. All those in attendance unanimously acknowledged that such audacious actions were indicative of a future leader, or sentiments to that effect.

Today, at the age of sixty-three, Narendra Modi reminisces about these events from over half a century ago with a casual shrug. With a twinkle in his eye, he simply states that his childhood was typical.

In conversations with former schoolmates and teachers, a prominent characteristic attributed to young Narendra was his quiet but unwavering determination. When he firmly believed in a particular conviction or course of action, he exhibited the common traits of childhood obstinacy and mischief. Nonetheless, to the delight of his parents,

Narendra's overall disposition was remarkably ordinary – he was a cheerful, energetic, and moderately popular child.

However, even in his normalcy, certain distinguishing qualities emerged. Foremost among these was Narendra's physical prowess. He was a wiry and athletic youngster. This aspect is noteworthy because early physical confidence can significantly influence one's self-perception. Despite having numerous childhood friends, there are scant recollections that attest to Narendra's sociability or a particular inclination towards team sports.

Today, Mr. Modi expresses his appreciation for cricket, albeit solely as a spectator, considering it a sport suited for contemplative individuals. Swimming, on the other hand, appealed to him during his childhood, but it inherently embodies a solitary pursuit. A hint of solitude persists in the anecdotes Mr. Modi shares about himself, wherein he is consistently present but often positioned on the periphery of gatherings and events, patiently awaiting the opportune moment to make a significant contribution to the unfolding narrative or drama.

Religion permeates every facet of Indian society, omnipresent and unassuming. The culture is deeply infused with religious elements, with myth, ritual, or their symbols interwoven into nearly every social activity and its significance. Religion in India seamlessly integrates with everyday life. It is plausible that certain characteristics exhibited by the young Narendra were perceived more as products of cultural influence rather than strictly religious ones.

During his youth, Narendra displayed early signs of asceticism, a trait that garnered significant attention from his family and acquaintances. Notably, he began by abstaining from the consumption of salt, followed by a renunciation of chillies and even oil. These self-imposed restrictions saw him relinquishing the typical pleasures of life, prompting one to ponder their underlying purpose. Narendra, reflecting on his past, humorously recalls that he still enjoyed jaggery but had forsaken it during his boyhood.

Such acts of renunciation and asceticism can be indicative of piety, but they may also signify ambition, often of a social nature. Initially, such endeavours can mirror a desire to attain a particular social status, akin to acquiring gentility as a precursor to pursuing further avenues of advancement.

It is plausible that Narendra embarked on his ascetic journey for rational and non-religious reasons. Internally, he sensed a distinctiveness that set him apart from others, a facet that frequently surfaced during our extensive conversations. Consequently, it seemed natural for him to probe and comprehend this sense of uniqueness by subtracting elements from his life that were commonly taken for granted by others. Through this process, he sought to 'normalize' his sensation of separateness and, in the process, unearth insights about himself.

For instance, this endeavor may have reassured him of his inner strength and lack of greediness. The practice of self-denial can be inherently self-revealing, aiding in the comprehension of one's individuality. In essence, it contributes to the development of character by fostering self-awareness and inner strength.

As he occupies his expansive office, with a terrace on one side and comfortable sofas on the other, Narendra Modi exudes a profound sense of tranquility when discussing his childhood and formative years. Nonetheless, he readily breaks into laughter when reminiscing about old memories. At his residence, he appears even more at ease, sharing, "There were times when, prior to my tenure as chief minister, I would go months and years without sharing a meal under the same roof!"

Narendra possessed a voracious appetite for reading, a quality that was notably tenacious, leading him to eschew the study of Sanskrit. His early devotion to Swami Vivekananda is well-documented, reflecting not only a spiritual connection but also an intellectual admiration for this 'ecumenical' figure. Swami Vivekananda's ability to reinterpret Hinduism for contemporary purposes, demonstrating its commonalities with other faiths through his 'enlightened liberalism,' left a lasting imprint on Narendra's worldview.

Young Narendra's conspicuous religiosity could potentially be attributed to his endeavor to categorize a particular form of behavior and personality that, during that era, was relatively unconventional within his social class and environment. In India, individuals who deviated from societal norms and sought spiritual meaning often gravitated towards gurus and ashrams, with the most fervent among them embracing the path of sadhus or monks. Traditionally, religion served as a receptacle for disruptive spiritual energy. However, Narendra charted his own course, a path challenging to decipher without the context of religious framing. It may have been an uncommon trait, but Narendra Modi was already an atypical young man.

It is evident and alluded to that Narendra was frequently eager to cooperate and offer assistance, to actively participate. Following his school hours, Narendra would eagerly rush to his father's tea stall, where it seemed as if working there was the very excitement he had anticipated all day. Serving tea to railway passengers held an unparalleled fulfilment for him. As he recounts, "I was in the train compartment, the small boy who used to serve tea, and take the money!"

In those days, it was customary for children to contribute to the family's business, regardless of its size, and they embraced this responsibility willingly. However, young Narendra harbored aspirations that extended beyond the norm—a desire to immerse himself in a broader, more mature world beyond the confines of the classroom. It raises the question of whether childhood held a special significance for him or if he found it somewhat uneventful and disinterested in typical play, preferring instead to seek knowledge and engage in activities beyond the customary expectations of a child.

When asked about his sentiments towards his childhood, Narendra Modi remains non-committal, stating, "By and large, everyone has a fondness for their childhood, and I was no exception."

Did Narendra's exceptional physical and mental strength lead him to perceive himself as more mature than his age? Did this self-concept, somewhat restrained by childhood, cultivate his interest in history, politics, a global perspective, and consequently, patriotism? Did it instill in him a deep respect for the past and an implicit desire to join the ranks of his elders?

In conjunction with his introspective nature and extensive reading, the evolution of such a self-identity could naturally kindle a sense of duty and belonging on a broader scale. Remarkably, Narendra was merely eight years old when he commenced attending the local shakha of the Rashtriya Swayamsevak Sangh (RSS), a pivotal decision that would chart the course of his life.

Reflecting on his birthplace, Gujarat, one may wonder about the hand of fate in shaping Narendra's life. India is a vast and diverse country, each region marked by its unique character. How might his upbringing and development have differed if he were a resident of Bihar or Bengal, for instance? To what extent did Gujarat, with its distinct culture, traditions, and sensibilities, influence the molding of Narendra Modi's character and ideals?

Gujarat boasts approximately one-third of India's total

coastline, a result of intricate coastal features, including inlets, folds, and bays. This geographical disposition has historically inclined the state towards the political Right, primarily due to the deep-rooted trading and business culture among Gujaratis, which has thrived along their extensive coastline for countless generations.

Across the Arabian Sea, one encounters emirates, caliphates, and kingdoms that have served as both commercial partners and competitors with Gujarat for centuries, pre-dating the arrival of Muslims in India as conquerors and settlers. This robust exchange of goods naturally led to the influx of traders and laborers from both directions. Arabs and Muslims, predominantly of the Sunni denomination, have established longstanding communities in Gujarat. The maritime nature of trade has fostered an adventurous, exploratory spirit and a business-oriented ethos among Gujaratis of diverse faiths, who have, in turn, established commercial footholds worldwide. Today, the quintessential British corner shop is an institution synonymous with the Gujarati community, while in the United States, motels have become an almost generic representation of Gujarati entrepreneurship.

Gujarat's rich mercantile heritage is distinctly reflected in its aesthetics, characterized by an Arabic influence evident in its colors, designs, and traditional costumes, particularly in regions like Saurashtra and the southern part of the state. Delving further into its historical roots and examining the adornments and features of certain tribal communities, one can discern even faint traces of African influence. Notably, Gujaratis were among the earliest Indians to engage in trade with and establish settlements in East Africa, a testament to their adaptive cultural acumen.

Unlike residents of landlocked states, Gujaratis are inherently outward-looking and open to diverse influences. They exhibit a remarkable receptivity to other cultures and communities.

For instance, the Parsis, who sought refuge from present-day Iran nearly 1,400 years ago, found a safe haven in Gujarat, illustrating the state's long-standing tradition of offering sanctuary to those in need.

The state of Gujarat stands out not only for its trade and external interactions but also for the profound impact of commerce within its own towns and villages on its political landscape. Unlike many other regions in India, the ripple effects of events in Gujarat's towns were swiftly felt in its rural areas, and vice versa. This was primarily due to the enduring presence of a vibrant business culture that, over centuries, fostered an exceptional level of communication between urban and rural areas. This vibrant connectedness was reflected in an extensive network of roads, facilitating mobility and engagement.

This culture of connectivity and market-friendliness in Gujarat has contributed to a distinctive ethos of individuality and entrepreneurship while simultaneously nurturing a sense of shared identity among its people. Over time, this duality has proven to be both an asset and a challenge. It has energized the state when communal conflicts arose, and then promptly aided in the restoration of normalcy, allowing Gujarat to swiftly resume its bustling daily life.

Bengal presents a stark contrast to Gujarat, symbolizing a distinct ideological and temperamental orientation, often associated with the political Left. Its individuality is shaped differently, prioritizing political principles over profit, and this orientation seems to be rooted in both geography and history.

Historically, Kolkata, formerly known as Calcutta, served as the imperial capital of the British Raj until 1911. The legacy of colonial bureaucracy and its meticulous rigor may have permeated the Bengali temperament, leading to a sense of bereavement and frustration at the loss of authority through association, particularly at a time when revolutionary fervor was brewing in Russia.

In 1964, V.S. Naipaul remarked that "Calcutta was dead," attributing this decline to the severance of ties with the British Raj. He observed that the city, which had been the cradle of the Indian Renaissance and the birthplace of many prominent figures in Indian reform, had also become the site of a mutual estrangement. The expected cross-fertilization of ideas had not materialized, leading to a sense of disillusionment and a retreat into a glorified past—an escape into the realm of memory and identity, as opposed to embracing the future.

Kolkata, in many aspects, bears resemblance to Paris, another city known for its left-leaning disposition, marked by its spirited activism and romantic self-absorption. Kolkata's Howrah Bridge could be considered its counterpart to Paris's Eiffel Tower, while the Hooghly River that flows alongside it mirrors the charming ambiance of the Marais district along the Seine. Kolkata serves as the residence of India's intellectual elites, thinkers, poets, and high-art filmmakers, akin to how Paris's Left Bank has historically been a hub for France's artistic revolutionaries.

Similar to Paris, Kolkata carries an air of haughtiness and pride, often displaying an inward-looking perspective and a distinctive sense of style in its own right. Moreover, like the French, the city exhibits a proclivity for engaging in acts of sabotage, whether through its distinct political movements or cultural expressions.

If Narendra Modi had been born in Kolkata, given his inherent sense of being different, his preference for solitude, and his passion for reading, it's possible that he might have felt a stronger affinity with the city's cultural atmosphere. In such a scenario, he might have seamlessly assimilated into Kolkata's cultural fabric.

Perhaps, at an early stage, Narendra would have immersed himself in the cinema of Satyajit Ray, making a mark as a radical filmmaker or pursuing a career in photography, similar to the renowned Sunil Janah. Narendra's inherent wanderlust and affinity for cameras might have led him down this artistic path.

Given his rugged individuality, it's not entirely implausible to consider that he could have been drawn towards the orthodoxies of the Communist Party of India, aligning with a more left-leaning political ideology. Alternatively, he might have found inspiration in Rabindranath Tagore, choosing to reside simply at Shantiniketan and following Tagore's philosophies.

However, considering the opportunities and cultural context in Bengal, it's conceivable that Narendra could have evolved into a populist politician more akin to Mamata Banerjee. In this scenario, he might have emerged as a champion of the underprivileged, rather than the technocrat and modernizer that his Gujarati upbringing led him to become, implicitly believing in commerce and free markets.

Would Narendra Modi now be contending for the position of Prime Minister if he had not been deeply influenced by the same environment that nurtured figures like Mahatma Gandhi, Sardar Vallabhbhai Patel, and Muhammad Ali Jinnah? It appears improbable that his appeal, had it developed elsewhere, would have extended across so many state borders. The influence of one's environment is undeniable, shaping and limiting individuals in various ways.

While it's crucial to exercise caution when speculating about such intangibles, it remains of paramount importance to delve into the psychological impact of one's cultural environment, particularly for someone who could soon be entrusted with governing the destinies of over a billion people. Understanding these influences holds valuable insights into future conduct and decision-making.

CHAPTER 3

"Visionary Leadership: Narendra Modi's Journey and Parallel Paths with Dhirubhai Ambani"

History has proven that one of the characteristics of a great leader is having a vision. We all have a vision for this or that, but a good leader not only has a vision, but he is able to communicate his vision to those around him, whether it is for his organization or for society. As already mentioned, people don't follow others, they follow their idea of success. When Alexander landed on the lands of Asia and led his army to defeat the powerful Persian king Darius III, this feat earned praise not only from Alexander but also from the world power of Greece. But Alexander was the only one who saw this vision. . Conqueror of the World Likewise, when Gandhiji gave salt from the hands of a dandy or called for the closure of India, he was thinking only of his own idea of a free India, but his vision of a free India resonated with everyone . His actions were not seen as mere acts but part of a larger plan to liberate India from the British. An important part of defining a vision is clarity and simplicity. Managers of all types often face uncertainty and complexity. It is necessary to understand that vision is not something written down on paper, but rather becomes the basis for implementation. So a simple vision is not only clear and focused, but also delivers a clear message about what needs to be achieved along that vision. A vision is more than a leader's dream. Rather, it also provides guidance to those who respect the leader and decide which path to follow to achieve the vision. Having a clear vision for the future is perhaps the most important aspect of leadership. Leaders who are trusted by the public are always effective and therefore take greater responsibility for having a clear vision for the businesses they engage with. It helps provide direction, meaning, satisfaction and understanding to everyone who is part of the environment. Openness breeds understanding. Understanding leads to productivity, and productivity leads to cultivation, which makes us want the species to return. As independent India's most popular leader, Modi has established himself as a man with clear goals. He shares not only his kind voice but also his confidence in the dream of building an India focused on economic growth and better governance. His clear and long-term "successful" vision makes him a leader who can lead and drive much-needed change in India. Millions of Indians entrust Modi with this enormous responsibility because they can entrust him with a vision for India's future and good ideas and plans to make that vision a reality. Ahead of the 2014 Indian general elections, Modi's party, the Bharatiya Janata Party (BJP), emerged as the only party with a clear vision. The campaign's goals are also clear. The goal is to secure a majority by increasing the number of seats by at least 272. To realize this vision, we first released it to the party and the public under the name 'Project 272'. Effective leaders can attract followers by setting goals for achievement. Today, the people of India want change for the better, but they are confused by their government. Modi was chosen as the high representative because of his clear vision for India's future. Most people would agree that in the years before Modi, India lacked a clear vision for growth and development. Development is often linked to government programs or support structures. Business and governance models lack a clear vision for development because they focus on establishing national or collective governance. Modi has laid out a clear vision of reform that includes specific, if not general, processes. From a broader perspective, the Indian dream can be seen as a broad metaphor that underpins his motivations. He seems to have thought of all the important things he believes India needs to focus on to truly shine. His vision was broad and included everything from promoting agricultural research to building superior infrastructure and financial investments. The focus is on cities, education, reduction of corruption and inflation, job creation, skills development, technology and collaborative activities for efficiency. The 'Brand India' strategy, which supports the development of the 5 Ts (Culture, arts, tourism, technology and business), has also helped create the image of India being proud to stand alongside the world's developed economies. Modi used China as an example when talking about how the development of new cities can increase economic prosperity. This idea is very attractive to many people, especially business people, who are interested in politicians talking about infrastructure. The Ambani brothers, some of India's leading politicians, called Modi the "king of kings" and admired his grand vision and goals. Modi's vision is not only clear but also very effective: Everything he does or plans comes back to the same goal of "making India great".

This connection helps him connect with the vision of his target (people of India). So when you talk about better roads, better technology, better governance, every Indian citizen thinks this is necessary to make India great. An important aspect of vision is to provide a foundation for the vision. He talked about international countries like Japan and China and how they became leaders, thus setting India's ultimate goal of entering the same league. He has a good understanding of the governance of India as a whole, his 15 years of administration has given him a good understanding of issues at the grassroots level, hence his vision sells national and international issues as well as problems in society. His vision is not only the product of a dream that may be noisy in its execution, but it also has a basis of understanding, limitations, and a clear path to use.As Theodore Hesburg, president of the University of Notre Dame, said: "The essence of leadership is that you have a vision. It should be a vision that you can be clear and strong in every situation." Similarly, Narendra Modi always expresses his vision. Over time, this affirmation was reshaped not only in Modi himself but also in the hearts of his believers. Modi has set the development agenda from day one, making it a representative of people who can express their belief in development. He underlined the idea of continuous improvement and realized that people now equate Narendra Modi with growth and development. This is the essential characteristic of every leader and his words. This single-minded and transparent process worked to his advantage because it eliminated political discourse and redirected it towards his own development. When critics question his credentials in the region or his involvement in thought, they will not question his management or vision, thus spreading his critics' message and creating relationships with stakeholders who must play an important role in mass communication. His vision is not wrong because he has well articulated his ideas on achieving them. Speaking openly, he promoted India's economic development, the concept of clean government and the concept of "minimum government, maximum governance". It was considered part of his understanding of the problems plaguing the country and its economy. So when a leader is asked to come up with landmarks that will help solve problems that people can relate to, he is someone who has the trust of the crowd and that is the least problem with Narendra Modi.

Looking at Modi's early life, one can see parallels with his current life and his thoughts on defining the vision before moving forward. As a child, Modi wanted to escape the physical constraints of family life when he started attending the RSS-edited daily Shakha. He knew from the beginning that he was looking for a special character, he was impressed by the RSS discipline and other life, he was inspired by RSS leaders from the right. Modi is an example of a visionary leader. However, it is worth noting that this quality cannot be built overnight. A person does not think this way, especially if he is young and has not yet discovered this world. Modi also faced uncertainty and confusion about life in his later years as a teenager. Being a dedicated worker, he is able to explore his strengths and understand the way the world is going, which helps him create his own vision. He is not ashamed of even the most important tasks, as he only thinks about his long-term vision and knows that these are stepping stones to a better and stronger future. In the case of Gujarat, where Narendra Modi was chief minister from 2001 to 2014, the power of vision is clear. Its future plans are detailed and ambitious enough to help Gujarat by 2030. Changes brought about by state policies have led to investments in the state towards the development of Gujarat. Good growth. To encourage investment in Gujarat, Modi also announced the 'Vibrant Gujarat' Entrepreneurs Summit, organized by the Gujarat government every two years. Modi thinks Gujarat will become the hub of Asia and a platform for countries like China, Japan, Thailand and Sri Lanka. This is part of Modi's grand vision for Gujarat, known as the 'Gujarat Model'. This development model paid off in some respects and brought about a positive change in the state of Gujarat, making it one of the largest states in India. Whether it is agricultural development or economic expansion, Modi clearly explains their goals and explains how they plan to implement their ideas. This is probably the biggest reason why visions become reality. In 2000, Gujarat's agricultural GDP grew at 9.8%, compared to just 2% in 1990. As Modi leads the country as Prime Minister, outlining his vision for India, there is hope and confidence that India will be on track to achieve its goal. Size. He promised to end corruption, make India a manufacturing hub and ensure digital and financial inclusion. Modi's clear vision is also seen in breaking down all the goals into smaller, clearer goals, making it easier to understand where we are going. For example, when Modi said he was focusing on "clean India," he did so by making appointments (by 2019), organizing events (like holding the World Meet Toilet Summit in Delhi), and providing support from the government (more money) to do it. This goal appears to have been achieved. Money to build toilets). Similarly, to achieve the goal of becoming a smart and inclusive country, Modi proposed the goal of "Digital India", which aims to digitally transform India into a knowledge economy. Modi's clear vision is like a great magnet that keeps him moving forward. An important aspect of Modi's vision is that it is not only the essence of India today, but is also deeply rooted in Indian culture and what we strive for. What did our ancestors think? His vision is unique and has gone through all aspects of the Indian mind, from cleanliness to wisdom, becoming a global force and easily understood by men. Therefore, they appropriate this vision to themselves. It has been proven that great leaders who are successful around the world are motivated by a grand vision of what they want to do. Their goals are clear, which helps them stay on track and focus on the right things. Dhirubhai Ambani, businessman and founder of Reliance Industries, is an example of a leader who insists on vision and strategy. A man ahead of his time, he had the courage to realize limitless dreams, which is also the symbol of Narendra Modi. Dhirubhai transformed Reliance from a small business into a major private equity firm and a Fortune 500 company. This tremendous growth was possible because of his belief in having a larger than life vision. Modi's distinct ideas about India's growth and development are parallel with how Dhirubhai imagined the country to be. Convinced that India could become an economic superpower, he wanted Reliance to contribute towards this ideal. Both these leaders understood the importance of investment as a driving tool for development. While Dhirubhai was among the first to discover and believe in the untapped potential of capital markets, Modi has also been emphasizing on generating investments and improving basic infrastructure. Dhirubhai believes in the importance of keeping a vision in mind and also emphasizes the importance of "keeping up with the times". It is equally important to update these well-thought-out plans with new ideas and take progress into account. Modi exemplifies this when he sets plans and targets, adopts new practices and adapts them to accept top priority. Just like Dhirubhai, who came from humble beginnings but built a life full of outstanding achievements, Modi symbolizes following one's vision with confidence, courage and belief. An important similarity between the two leaders is that they have both charted a path for themselves and overcome challenges from established environments. Their vision is filled with creativity as they seek new ways to achieve their goals. While openly operating in a protectionist manner, Dhirubhai was able to follow the path of his neighbors who focused on protection and providing them with secure employment. Instead, he chooses to take advantage of today's opportunities and look to tomorrow. At that time, large companies were investing little in R&D or expertise, even improving their international competitiveness. So when the Indian market opened in 1991, most of them left. Dhirubhai's vision is not just a short-term goal (to publish today's results) but also a long-term goal: to be globally competitive. Similarly, Modi's vision is not short-term to achieve minor improvements in governance but long-term to make India globally competitive. They all constitute a combination of top-down and bottom-up approaches to consensus. Reliance built the Patalganga Refinery in record time in the eighties; It is not only a huge commercial success, but also a world-class facility for refining oil land at the cheapest price. Dhirubhai is well done with a vision for the future as he knows that the Trust will have to be at the forefront when one day India will have to open its markets. So he invested the year after the change. Similarly, Narendra Modi, who aims for the highest office, has been serving in the country since 2002-2003. Realizing the weakness of the BJP in the south of India, he began visiting these states from 2002 to 2003, where his speeches were translated into local languages and he delivered speeches reported in local newspapers. Similarly, it started to join the grassroots in Uttar Pradesh and Bihar, which are the important states that collect the most MPs in the Indian Parliament. Although his name rose to the top of the post only a decade later, his long-term vision and investment paid him great dividends; Uttar Pradesh and Bihar returned as BJP MPs in the 2014 Debate. Close to a third. Another similarity between Dhirubhai and Modi's vision is their strong economic outlook. We can attribute this to his famous Gujarati roots, but Dhirubhai's vision of creating value propositions for business owners and Modi's vision of bringing growth and economic prosperity for the people at large are interconnected and interconnected. Coming from humble beginnings, both men understood that success could only be achieved and be more beneficial to the relationship or organization if business benefits reached the lowest level of stakeholders. This approach makes it clear that leaders can be trusted by the public and members at large. These leaders are successful not because they have special status, special titles, or family connections, but because they choose to live their lives in a special way. They dare to dream, they carry a vision in their hearts and they work faithfully to realize this vision.

CHAPTER 4

Rise in Gujarat Politics and Development Leadership

Narendra Modi's entry into politics dates back to the early 1970s when he was a young man searching for his purpose. It was during this time that he decided to join the Rashtriya Swayamsevak Sangh (RSS), a prominent Hindu nationalist organization.

Within the RSS, Modi assumed the role of a pracharak, which meant he became a full-time worker for the organization. His responsibilities included propagating the RSS ideology and establishing connections with people across various regions of India. This phase of his life demanded immense dedication, as he traveled extensively to engage with people at the grassroots level.

Modi's time in the RSS proved instrumental in shaping his political journey. He gained valuable experience in organizational skills and developed strong relationships with individuals who shared his vision for the nation. These formative years laid the groundwork for his future in politics.

Joining the RSS marked the initial step in Narendra Modi's remarkable political career. The principles and knowledge he acquired during this period would serve as the foundation for his rise in Indian politics. This journey eventually propelled him to the position of Prime Minister of India, a role he has held since 2014.

Narendra Modi, the current Prime Minister of India, has had a long and varied political career that began in the early 1980s. His journey in politics is marked by several key experiences and roles that have shaped his political persona. In this detailed study, we will explore Modi's early political experiences and the roles he played during that period.

Early political experiences and roles

1. **Entry into Politics:** Narendra Modi's entry into politics was gradual. He was initially drawn to the Rashtriya Swayamsevak Sangh (RSS), a right-wing Hindu nationalist organization, during his teenage years. In the early 1970s, he became a full-time pracharak (campaigner) for the RSS, dedicating his time to the organization's activities. This marked his initial involvement in the political sphere.

2. **Role in the BJP:** Modi's association with the Bharatiya Janata Party (BJP) began in the mid-1980s. His organizational skills and dedication to the RSS made him a prominent figure within the BJP. He held various organizational positions within the party, including General Secretary and National Secretary, which allowed him to establish himself as a key strategist and a crucial figure in the party's inner circle.

3. **Campaign Management:** One of the defining features of Narendra Modi's early political career was his exceptional talent for campaign management. In the late 1980s and early 1990s, he played a pivotal role in the BJP's election campaigns. His meticulous planning and execution of campaigns in Gujarat and other states garnered attention and praise within the party.

4. **Chief Minister of Gujarat:** Narendra Modi's most significant early political role came in 2001 when he was appointed as the Chief Minister of Gujarat. This role would prove to be a turning point in his career. Under his leadership, Gujarat saw significant economic growth, infrastructure development, and a focus on industrialization. However, his tenure

was marred by controversies, including the handling of the 2002 Gujarat riots, which generated both criticism and support.

5. **Visionary Leadership:** Modi's time as Chief Minister of Gujarat showcased his visionary leadership style. He emphasized economic reforms, attracting investments, and improving the state's infrastructure. His "Vibrant Gujarat" summits became a platform for attracting business leaders and investment to the state, helping to bolster Gujarat's economy.

6. **Ideological Commitment:** Throughout his early political career, Modi remained committed to the ideological principles of the BJP and the RSS. His unwavering dedication to Hindutva, a term associated with Hindu nationalism, and his belief in strong national security resonated with the party's core base.

7. **National Recognition:** Narendra Modi's national recognition grew steadily during his tenure as Chief Minister of Gujarat. He became a prominent figure in national politics and was seen as a potential candidate for the role of Prime Minister.

8. **Prime Ministerial Candidacy and Victory:** In 2014, Modi was chosen as the BJP's candidate for the Prime Minister's position. His campaign, centred around the promise of economic development and good governance, led to a historic victory in the general elections. He became the 14th Prime Minister of India and was re-elected for a second term in 2019.

Narendra Modi's early political experiences and roles laid the foundation for his ascent to becoming the Prime Minister of India. His journey from a dedicated RSS pracharak to a powerful Chief Minister and ultimately to the highest office in the land is a testament to his political acumen, organizational skills, and unwavering commitment to his party's ideology. His leadership continues to shape India's political landscape, making him a pivotal figure in contemporary Indian politics.

Early Political Career in Gujarat

Narendra Modi's journey in Gujarat's political landscape began in the late 1980s and evolved significantly over the years.

1. **Entry into Politics:** Modi's entry into politics happened after he joined the Rashtriya Swayamsevak Sangh (RSS) in his youth. His association with the RSS, a right-wing nationalist organization, provided him with a foundation in ideological and organizational skills, which would later prove invaluable in his political career.

2. **Rapid Rise within the BJP:** In 1987, Narendra Modi took his first significant step into active politics when he was appointed as the General Secretary of the Gujarat unit of the Bharatiya Janata Party (BJP). This marked his formal entry into mainstream politics in Gujarat.

3. **Role in Advani's Rath Yatra:** During the late 1980s and early 1990s, Modi played a prominent role in L.K. Advani's Rath Yatra, a political campaign aimed at rallying support for the construction of a Ram Temple at Ayodhya. His organizational skills and ability to mobilize party workers were evident during this period.

4. **Becoming Chief Minister:** Narendra Modi's big break came in 2001 when he was appointed as the Chief Minister of Gujarat. This appointment came at a challenging time for the state, as it was reeling from a devastating earthquake. Modi's leadership

and governance style during this period laid the foundation for his future in Gujarat politics.

5. **Re-elections and Development Focus:** Modi went on to be re-elected as Chief Minister in 2002, 2007, and 2012. His tenure as Chief Minister was marked by a strong focus on economic development and industrialization in Gujarat. The state witnessed impressive growth in sectors such as petrochemicals and infrastructure.

6. **National Prominence:** His tenure as Chief Minister brought him considerable national attention. While his economic policies received praise, his handling of the 2002 Gujarat riots remained a subject of controversy and debate.

7. **Stepping onto the National Stage:** Narendra Modi's leadership in Gujarat eventually propelled him to the national stage. In 2013, he was selected as the BJP's prime ministerial candidate for the 2014 general elections.

8. **Legacy:** Modi's legacy in Gujarat is a mix of economic development and political polarization. His tenure as Chief Minister saw Gujarat emerge as an economic powerhouse, but it was also marred by the controversies surrounding the 2002 riots.

Narendra Modi's early political career in Gujarat was marked by a steady rise within the BJP, his role in critical political events, and his eventual ascension to the position of Chief Minister. His influence and impact on Gujarat's political landscape are undeniable, and they set the stage for his subsequent journey to becoming the Prime Minister of India.

Becoming Chief Minister Of Gujrat

Narendra Modi's journey to becoming the Chief Minister of Gujarat was a significant milestone in his political career. Let's delve into the details of this crucial phase:

In 2001, Gujarat was grappling with the aftermath of a devastating earthquake that had caused immense loss of life and infrastructure. The Bharatiya Janata Party (BJP), recognizing the need for strong leadership during this challenging time, appointed Narendra Modi as the Chief Minister of the state.

Modi's appointment as Chief Minister came as a surprise to many, as he was relatively unknown on the national political stage. However, his organizational skills, dedication, and his reputation as a disciplined and efficient administrator within the BJP played a crucial role in his selection.

Upon assuming office, Modi wasted no time in implementing his vision for Gujarat's development. He focused on attracting investments, promoting industrial growth, and improving the state's infrastructure. His administration introduced various policies and initiatives to create a business-friendly environment, which led to Gujarat becoming one of India's most prosperous states.

Under Modi's leadership, Gujarat witnessed significant advancements in sectors such as petrochemicals, textiles, and manufacturing. The state became a hub for investment, attracting both domestic and international companies. Modi's emphasis on infrastructure development resulted in the construction of world-class roads, ports, and industrial parks, further boosting Gujarat's economic growth.

Modi's governance style was characterized by efficiency, transparency, and a hands-on approach. He implemented innovative measures to streamline bureaucratic processes, reduce corruption, and improve the delivery of public services. His administration also prioritized the welfare of farmers, implementing policies to support agricultural growth and enhance rural development.

However, Modi's tenure as Chief Minister was not without controversy. The 2002 Gujarat riots, which occurred shortly after he assumed office, remain a dark chapter in his political career. The riots resulted in significant loss of life, property, and communal tensions. Critics have accused Modi of not doing enough to prevent the violence and of mishandling the aftermath. The incident continues to be a subject of debate and criticism.

Despite the controversies, Modi's popularity within Gujarat remained strong. He was re-elected as Chief Minister in 2002, 2007, and 2012, each time with a resounding mandate. His ability to connect with the masses, his charismatic leadership style, and his focus on development resonated with the people of Gujarat.

Modi's tenure as Chief Minister of Gujarat laid the foundation for his subsequent rise to the national stage. His success in transforming Gujarat into an economic powerhouse and his reputation as a decisive leader propelled him to become the Prime Minister of India in 2014.

Narendra Modi's journey to becoming the Chief Minister of Gujarat was marked by his ability to navigate through challenging circumstances, his focus on development, and his strong leadership skills. While his tenure brought significant economic growth to the state, it was also marred by the controversies surrounding the 2002 riots. Nonetheless, his achievements in Gujarat set the stage for his larger political ambitions and his eventual role as the Prime Minister of India.

Policies and initiatives for Gujrat Development

Narendra Modi, during his tenure as the Chief Minister of

Gujarat from 2001 to 2014, implemented a range of policies and initiatives aimed at fostering the economic and social development of the state. These initiatives had a significant impact on various sectors, including agriculture, industry, infrastructure, and education. Let's delve into some of the key policies and initiatives:

1. **Vibrant Gujarat Summit:** Modi initiated the Vibrant Gujarat Summit in 2003, which brought together business leaders, policymakers, and investors from around the world. This event showcased Gujarat as an investment-friendly destination and led to numerous MoUs and investments in the state

2. **Industrial Growth:** Under Modi's leadership, Gujarat became a hub for industrial development. The state introduced policies such as "Single Window Clearance" to streamline the approval process for setting up businesses. This attracted major industries like automobile manufacturing, petrochemicals, and textiles.

3. **Agricultural Reforms:** To boost the agricultural sector, Modi introduced innovative schemes like Sardar Patel Sahakari Urja Yojana, which aimed at providing reliable electricity to rural areas. Additionally, the Krishi Mahotsav initiative promoted modern agricultural practices and improved crop yields.

4. **Infrastructure Development:** Gujarat saw substantial improvements in infrastructure during Modi's tenure. The state invested in road networks, ports, and power generation. The development of the Mundra Port, for example, transformed it into one of India's largest commercial ports.

5. **Education and Skill Development:** Modi prioritized education and skill development through initiatives like "Vidya Lakshmi" and "Kaushalya Vardhan Kendra." These programs aimed to enhance the quality of education and equip the youth with employable skills.

6. **Renewable Energy:** Gujarat became a leader in renewable energy production under Modi's leadership. Initiatives like the Solar Power Policy encouraged the development of solar energy projects, making the state a pioneer in the sector.

7. **Women's Empowerment:** Modi launched schemes like "Kanya Kelavani" and "Maa Annapurna Yojana" to empower women through education and nutrition.

8. **Urban Development:** The Swarnim Jayanti Mukhya Mantri Shaheri Vikas Yojana focused on improving urban infrastructure and housing for the urban poor.

9. **Disaster Management:** Gujarat's efforts in disaster management, especially during the 2001 earthquake and subsequent floods, were recognized for their effectiveness in minimizing loss of life and property.

10. **Good Governance:** Modi's administration emphasized good governance and transparency through e-governance initiatives like "e-Gram Vishwagram" and "SWAGAT," which enhanced public service delivery.

Narendra Modi's policies and initiatives during his tenure as the Chief Minister of Gujarat played a pivotal role in the state's development. They contributed to Gujarat's transformation into an economic powerhouse and a model for inclusive growth. These efforts laid the foundation for many of the national policies he later implemented as the Prime Minister of India.

Economic and social changes in Gujarat during his tenure

During Narendra Modi's tenure as the Chief Minister of Gujarat from 2001 to 2014, the state witnessed significant economic and social changes. These changes were often attributed to his leadership and the policies implemented during his tenure.

Economic Changes:

1. **Industrial Growth:** One of the key aspects of Modi's tenure was the emphasis on industrial growth. He actively promoted Gujarat as an investment-friendly destination, which attracted both domestic and foreign investors. As a result, industries such as manufacturing, textiles, and petrochemicals saw substantial growth.

2. **Infrastructure Development:** Under Modi's leadership, Gujarat witnessed a massive improvement in infrastructure. The state invested in building roads, ports, and power plants, which not only facilitated industrial growth but also improved the overall quality of life for the people.

3. **Agriculture:** While industrialization was a priority, agriculture wasn't neglected. Modi's government worked on improving irrigation facilities and providing better access to credit for farmers, leading to increased agricultural productivity.

4. **Gujarat's GDP Growth:** During Modi's tenure, Gujarat consistently recorded high GDP growth rates, often surpassing the national average. This economic growth was driven by a pro-business environment, efficient administration, and a focus on development.

5. **Education:** Efforts were made to improve the education sector. Many new schools and colleges were established, and initiatives were launched to increase literacy rates and the quality of education in the state.

6. **Healthcare:** The healthcare sector also saw improvements. New hospitals and medical facilities were set up, and healthcare services were made more accessible to the rural population.

7. **Women's Empowerment:** Various schemes were launched to empower women, including financial assistance for self-help groups and initiatives to improve female literacy and reduce maternal mortality.

8. **Rural Development:** Modi's tenure saw a focus on rural development. Programs were initiated to provide basic amenities to rural areas, including drinking water, electricity, and sanitation.

9. **Urbanization:** The urban areas of Gujarat underwent significant development with modern amenities and better living conditions. Cities like Ahmedabad saw major infrastructural transformations.

10. **Social Harmony:** Gujarat, which had faced communal tensions in the past, experienced relative social harmony during Modi's tenure. Efforts were made to promote religious tolerance and maintain law and order.

It's important to note that opinions on Modi's tenure in Gujarat are divided. While some see it as a period of rapid economic growth and development, others have raised concerns about issues like environmental degradation and social inequalities. Additionally, critics have pointed out that the benefits of economic growth may not have reached all sections of society equally.

Narendra Modi's time as Chief Minister of Gujarat was marked by significant economic and social changes. His leadership style, focus on industrialization, and infrastructure development played a pivotal role in shaping the state's progress during his tenure. However, it's essential to consider various perspectives and the long-term impact of these changes on the people of Gujarat.

CHAPTER 5

"Modi's Visionary Governance: Navigating Challenges, Inspiring Change"

Leaders have many advantages, especially vision and responsibility for our country's future. Our president is a great orator. Be it his historic Independence Day speech in 2014 or many other important events in the country, he always comes up with something new and powerful and provides solutions to thousands of unresolved problems. For decades. In this section, we have tried to include his motivational quotes and answers to riddles found around the country. In one of his speeches, he focused on the need for change in the country's infrastructure. He said: "In infrastructure, the focus needs to shift from highways to i-ways and fiber networks. Previously, cities were built on river banks. Now they are being built along highways. But going forward, it will be built on the availability of fiber networks and next-generation infrastructure." "And think about the national goals: 'Ek Bharat, Bharat' Modi." Shreshtha added. The prime minister told leaders that overcoming political ideologies and ignoring accusations of victory or defeat was key to progress. "We have to think about 'Rashtra'. Hit. Rashtraniti," the Prime Minister said, mentioning four ways to develop our country. Modi, a governance expert, believes that successful policies help in development. But the prime minister's main concern is the rapid growth of the economy. He believes in speed. In Modi's words, "Swarajya mila, lekin surajya nahin de paaye" (We have freedom, but we do not have good governance). Modi believes that misgovernance in a country can be worse than diabetes in an individual and can cause harm to the entire body. In one of his powerful speeches, he said, "Last mile delivery is the biggest challenge. The trust of all citizens of the country has been destroyed. It needs to be restored," Modi Max said. One of his virtues is devotion not to any political party, country or individual, but to the nation as a whole. He said that a nation is more than a political entity. Consignment. He also promised to rally support from all political parties in the country. Modi believes in the power of hard work. This raises awareness of the importance of recognizing employees and their value in society. The coach rejected the idea of granting a free pass. He said: "The way we treat our employees is a psychological issue and we need to make an effort to change that. Shrameva Jayate is an effort. We called ourselves "Fraudulent India". As the Indian Prime Minister said, Prime Minister Modi's visit to small neighbors like Nepal has received global recognition. "We welcome neighbors who feel free in our experiences. We want Nepal's development to reach the peak of the Himalayas," Modi said. Article Modi's powerful message: "The Constitution unites, not divides. Article This is not just a book. Past, present and future are mixed. "The Constitution of India is alive. It connects the Himalayas with the sea. It connects the vast Kutch Desert with lush greenery. Constitution of Nagaland," PM Modi said in his speech. "I can't believe it. However, the Indian Constitution was eventually abolished. "He brought hope to more than 125 million Indians and promised to realize their aspirations." According to Modi, "Hindi has old words that are still believed by most people in the country. "Pani aur Jawani Pahad Ke Kaam Nahi Aati" (Water and youth are useless in the mountains). But we are working hard to change these old beliefs.

Today, we must focus on how youth and water can be beneficial for hilly regions."

In his Independence Day speech, Modi emphasised on promoting tourism in India. He explained how important tourism is for the betterment of country and reducing levels of poverty. "Tourism provides employment to the poorest of the poor. earns Gram seller something, auto-rickshaw driver earns something, pakoda seller earns something, and tea seller also earns something. When there is talk of tea seller, I feel a sense of belongingness," Modi said in his speech.

Parliament sessions in India are a common tradition. Comments, quotes, speeches, criticisms, and planning, a lot takes place here. However, there is something more that the Prime Minister wants this place to do for the countrymen and welfare of the country in all. The Prime Minister said that sharp comments can give us space short time for a but cannot impact or inspire. He said the time had come when every sentence said in Parliament should be an inspiration for the country.

The country really needs a Prime Minister like Modi who are in service for the citizens present for day the and always. On the auspicious day of Independence of India, Modi had declared openly that he is the Servant of people of India. "I am present amidst you. not as the Prime Minister, but as the Prime Servant. The day of Independence is a festival when we take a solemn pledge of working for the welfare of mother India, and also for the welfare of the poor, oppressed, Dalits, the exploited and the backward people of our country," Narendra Modi said.

As per the opinion of the Prime Minister, the significance of a national festival is that of an occasion to purify and reconstruct the character of nation. It fills one with inspiration to pledge towards leading a life that refines one's character further. The festival also motivates one to devote oneself to the nation. Each action taken should be directly associated to the development and wellbeing of nation. This is how, according to Modi, Independence Day, the festival of freedom will transform into a festival of inspiration to help country reach out to newer heights.

Another management quality that gives our Prime edge

Minister over an other ministers is the willingness to serve and give countrymen their due credit. In one of his inspiring speeches, Modi had given full credit to his people and their day to day contributions. "My dear countrymen, this nation has neither been built by political leaders nor by rulers nor by governments. This nation has been built by our farmers, our workers, our mothers and sisters, our youth. The country has reached here today because of generation to generation rigours undertaken by Our sages, our saints, our maestros, our teachers, our scientists and social workers. These great people and these great generations, who had worked for the country throughout their lives, deserve our deepest respect," said Modi, in an attempt to honour the trymen of India.

When it comes to working towards the welfare each of nation, person is competent and powerful. He stated, "Right from a peon to the Cabinet Secretary everybody is capable. Everybody has power and experience. I want to harness their power and use it to speed up national welfare. I will certainly do it."

The leader had expressed his earnest gratitude towards the great men of India from the past who have laid their lives to get freedom. "We owe a lot to them," he says.

India is a country with powerful population of 125 crore people. Modi believes that this is one of the biggest assets for the nation and each citizen of India must make his share of contribution. "Everything is not for self interest only. There are certain things which are meant for the country and we have to refine this national character," says Modi. The Prime Minister is concerned about security of women in India. The increasing amount of rape and molestation cases in the country has created many problems. Here, Modi has a different vision than the rest of the political world. The Prime Minister has a different way to solve this problem. He urged the citizens of country to change their perspective towards boys and a major transformation in their upbringing style. "Parents ask their daughters hundreds of questions, but have any parents ever dared to ask their son as to where he is going, why he is going out, who his friends are? After all, a rapist is also somebody's son. He also has parents. As parents, have we ever asked our son as to what he is doing and where he going?" Modi says. Communal violence is something Modi had always been criticised for. Gujarat riots are the apparent reason behind this. In one of his speeches, Modi criticised the existence of communal violence across the nation. "Even after independence we sometimes face the poison of casteism or communalism. How long will it continue and who is going to benefit from it? I appeal to the youth of the country that the poison of casteism or communalism is a hindrance to Our country's progress. Think and try a ten years moratorium to get a society free of all these tensions," Modi said about communal violence.

Service to the nation, according to Modi can be in any form. He believes that a farmer from village also serves the country by filling the granaries. Similarly, a soldier defends the motherland through his services. Each of these duties is considered as a national service.

Less of importing items to the country is what Modi preaches. Here, the Prime Minister has come up with a new solution. He suggests each youth make at least one article that the country imports. This way, the article may never be imported in future.

Cleanliness in India

It is a big problem. It not only makes the country look bad but also results in many serious diseases. Modi has a very unique approach to the same. "If 125 crore countrymen decide not to ever spread filth, then no power in the world can make our village or town dirty," he said. What a brilliant leader he is!

Working hard is something Modi believes in and never shirk away from taking a step ahead for the betterment of country. However, he wants the entire country to work together. "I can promise you. If you work 12 hours, I will work for 13. Why? Because I am not a pradhan mantri, but a pradhan sevak," Modi says to instil the feeling of labour and efforts in each countryman.

Scientists contribute a lot to our country. Modi says that Vedas were scripted many centuries back in India. However, nobody knows who wrote them. Those rishis must have been great scientists of their own era and had a scientific approach to life. The modern scientists also contribute a lot to the society. "They meditate inside a laboratory and forget about their family. The scientists sacrifice a lot and dedicate their whole lives to invent something new to contribute to human welfare," says Modi.

Prime Minister of India holds great respect for the farmers.

Their contribution to the country is immense. "Our farmers can make gold out of mud, if they have sufficient supply of water," stated Modi.

Emphasising progress on of the nation, Modi says, "For any country progress, to infrastructure is of primary importance and automatically leads to development. In all infrastructure projects, power is most important."

Energy is very important to the country. Modi reminded people of the importance of the sun god in India. "We worship the sun god. He is always depicted with seven horses, and the horses of the sun god appear in the form of many powers that we can create for ourselves. I see a new image of these words in modern society. Through his articles, he conveyed to the leaders and convinced the citizens of India that the focus was on the development of power in the country and that this had been the responsibility of the government from the beginning. "We need to protect our pockets from high electricity bills. If your monthly bill is INR 90, it is your responsibility as a citizen to save around INR 10. The money you save can help you bring milk to your kids. Now is the time to spread the word. I realize it," explains Modi. According to the Prime Minister, patriotism is not just about fighting across borders. Saving electricity is also a service to the country. Your income will help you organize your monthly family budget. This helps us and all regular people. Saving energy helps everyone around you. What a great idea! Modi is a leader who not only tells people what to do, but also helps them learn how to do it. Every problem has a solution. He urged citizens to make efforts to contribute to energy conservation. You should start by turning off the lights in your home at night and enjoying its beauty. This saves energy. He urged Indian citizens to come out and enjoy the beauty of nature. • "Injustice destroys a nation," Modi said. The Prime Minister said that articles on corruption have become a good practice in the society. "I am with you to eradicate corruption once and for all. Some people get worried when we talk about corruption, but we must know that the people of India stand up and want a corruption-free country. "With your blessings, we will be able to eradicate this disease," the president promised. Modi believes that the development of any country depends on its people. Every developed country in the world has citizens who are determined to move forward and help their country develop. Joint action is the key to faster development for all countries. "If our people drove out the British and achieved independence, would we be able to escape poverty with 1.5 billion rupees?" – asked Modi. According to Modi, urban development is always seen as a limitation, problem and challenge by people. But the prime minister sees this as an opportunity. He said that now is the time to realize the importance of urban development. Special efforts must be made to generate new and consistent ideas. It takes a lot of time to complete the task. It is also necessary to ensure that the work is completed on time.

A breakthrough is very necessary.

Progressive nation is one that works with its citizens. Modi asserts that the people of nation should be willing to work hard for the nation's progress. Those who blame their destinies to have born in India will never get anything. Regardless of which part of the world one lives, it is important to respect one's roots. This is extremely important.

"Lord Rama visited Lanka, the city of Gold. He was a human being. Anybody could have strayed. But all he had to say was 'Swargadapi Gariyasi'. This is what he felt for Ayodhya. Regardless of how poor my Ayodhya is and the number of problems it has, for me, it is 'Swargadapi Gariyasi'. This is the biggest lesson we all must says. learn," Modi.

Whichever part of the world we are in, it is important to have at least one meal together. Having conversation in our national language is also crucial. Faith is very powerful. It is a kind of chemical and stronger than fevicol. It works towards making bonds stronger. Modi emphasises on the fact that developing states is crucial to ensure and steady speedy and progress of the country.

For Narendra Modi, a country is an organisation and its states, various teams. An organisation can progress only when all of its teams work together without any hostility among them. Similarly, the Prime Minister of India and Chief Ministers of various states (regardless of which party they belong to) must work together as one team.

"If we need to take the Indian economy forward then the purchasing power of the village people will have to be increased. This will impact the economic situation of cities," says Modi.

In one of his powerful speeches, the Prime Minister asked soft drink makers such as Pepsi to mix 5 per cent fruit juice with aerated drinks.

He says that this will help distressed farmers discover a brand new market for their manufacture. "We drink Pepsi, Coca-Cola and I do not know how many similar beverages are available in the market. The trade runs into billions of rupees. I have asked the companies if they can blend 5 per cent natural fruit juice in the beverages they make. I am not asking for much. If 5 per cent of juice from fruits produced by our farmers is added, farmer will the not be forced to search for a market to sell. A single decision can ensure billions of rupees of trade," Modi said.

"Swami Vivekananda had once predicted that India will turn into a Vishwa Guru. Swami Vivekananda's words have come true, I see it here. Mother India has actually become Vishwa Guru. She is represented all over the world through all of you, and you carry immense capacity. This foresight of Swami Vivekananda has come true," says Modi.

Faith is the most important thing. We have lost faith in our brothers. Now is the time to trust the government. Chinese people have the right to ask and discuss all important questions. "The message from our government is that we must trust every Indian. Places of trust can change a lot. However, this does not mean that the law will be changed in the National Assembly. Modi is confident that efforts are being made to resolve the situation beyond Parliament. Example"We must see the potential of every citizen of India. The faster the Indian middle class grows in numbers, the faster it collapses and the faster the poor are replaced by the rich. In other words, it is about becoming a company that is beneficial to the world." Faster." What should we do to grow the middle class? The immediate answer is: It has to be a job. If we leave the city and ignore economic development, manufacturing, and job creation, the cycle will not close. The Prime Minister believes in the power of yoga. According to him, "Yoga is a precious gift of our ancient traditions. Yoga represents the unity of mind and body. thoughts and actions; care and care; harmony between humans and nature; It's a great way to improve your health and fitness. This is not a movement, but a pursuit of understanding of oneself, the world and nature. "He urged people to work hard to establish an 'International Day of Yoga' and spare no efforts to achieve this goal. Modi's faith in power. He prayed for nine days during Navratri and fasting." Indian leaders believe that this festival is a celebration of self-purification and the development of the power of human passion. Modi believes that a mass movement can change India's course. He promised to work for the good of the country and not do anything that could lead the country to bankruptcy. What motivates Modi and gives him hope for a better India? "The power of 1.25 billion citizens" is his greatest strength and will help him achieve his goal of making India a better place and moving the country forward. The issue of Ganga cleaning is also one that Modi hopes to solve for his citizens. Then the sisters said: "Tell my brothers. Do you believe that the Ganges River can be made clean? Thousands of trillions of rupees have been withdrawn from banks and the people want to know why you did it. How can we get the Ganges River back to normal? When, how, and yes, for whom?

Modi had confessed that many of his acquaintances have advised him not to take up such difficult and impossible tasks. However, he paid no heed to these so called 'recommendations'.

According to Modi, "If it is just the simpler things he should focus on, then why had he been appointed as a Prime. Minister? It is certainly to undertake and accomplish the hardest of tasks and unresolved issues for decades that people have voted for Modi."

Youth Power is one of the biggest of all powers that exist in the country. This is what Modi believes in. He feels that India holds the strength and support of around 80 crore youths. And this is enough for any nation to progress towards success development. "I will fulfil the hopes of poor in India. My duty is to do everything that is required for the betterment of the nation. Right from providing clean water to each corner of the country to better healthcare facilities, and housing provisions, I will do all that it takes to see a better, developed, and India," promised. progressive Modi.

Prime Minister Narendra Modi was very hopeful on the official launch of his nationwide cleanliness campaign, the 'Swachh Bharat Mis-sion'(Clean India Campaign). "I have also started a social media campaign, I have invited nine people to post pictures of them cleaning and they will invite another nine people. This will create a whole new tradition. I hope you will help me take this work forward," said.

Modi. Buying Khadi can help us fetch food for the poor. Modi motivates his countrymen to buy at least one Khadi product for home or office. It may be anything from a handkerchief to a bed sheet. It will help improve India's economy to a great extent. The dynamic power of people in India is what Swami Vivekanada believed in many decades ago. This is what Modi belives in too. He feels that the progress of country is possible if 125 crore Indians work together. Serving Mother India should be the sole motive of the citizens to enjoy a better tomorrow.

Modi has introduced the five Ts that would be the focus of building Brand India: Technology, Tourism, Tradition, Trade and Talent. On the basis of the above mentioned Ts, the government and citizens together can take the country forward. "The country doesn't need an act. It demands action!" says Modi. "I hope for a united and happy nation from Kashmir to Kanyakumari." His biggest challenge is to add life' to the term 'file'.

"We are snake no longer charmer. We are now (Computer) mouse charmers," says Modi. For Modi, mission is everything in life. Ambitions hold no importance. He confessed that the dedication for work would have been of the same level while working as a municipal officer.

"I did not become CM on 17-10-2001. I was always a CM. By CM, I don't mean Chief Minister, but a Common Modi stated. Man,"

The Prime Minister believes that the government has only one religion 'India First'. Constitution is the religious book of government. Our Prime Minister is always on the lookout for something unique and revolutionary. This is what he has come up for the provision of people across the nation while voting.

According to Modi, "If there is one important issue even today, it is to further increase voter registration. The past several elections across India have seen record turnouts. This is a positive sign but there remain several people, particularly youngsters, who despite being eligible, are not registered as voters. The Election Commission has been extremely proactive in increasing registration but with more help from citizens, we can go even further."

Mobile Kiosks is one of the new plans he came up with. "We need to think about strengthening voter facilitation through innovative means such as mobile registration kiosks," Modi said.

Modi also emphasised on the need of online voting process India. "Further, we need to use mobile technology for voter registration, information dissemination about polling booths etc. It is also time we start discussing the possibilities of online voting, though admittedly it has its inherent challenges," Modi explained. Modi is looking for a team that can work towards the progress of India. "I want a Team India where the

Prime Minister and the Chief Ministers work together," says Modi. He says that his vast experience as a Chief Minister of Gujarat makes him believe in the power of team India. Enmity and differences within states can be a big problem. Each state should welcome people from other states and help them. 1+1 = 2. However, Modi wants to move a step ahead than this. The power of India when I meets make II.

Modi's another focus towards a progressive India is to provide employment. This is extremely necessary for the development of India. In an amusing statement, Modi says that the tradition of importing even the smallest things to India must be given a full stop. "We import tear gas to India. We even import tear gas shells. Even tears have to be imported. We have to change it. Why should an outsider make us weep? We can weep on our own," Modi said in an amusing tone.

Girl child must be honoured and given their due credit according to Modi. He condemns the tradition of sex determination and abortion of female foetuses.

The Prime Minister of India feels that special steps should be taken to eradicate the feeling of disrespect for girl child from the root.

Hard labour according to the Prime Minister of India is the key to success. Many a problem can be solved by by making dedicated efforts together. Cursing the fate is something most people do. However, it leads to nothing other than misery, hopelessness and tons of problems. Believing what one can do and working towards a goal is very important.

According to Modi, the government officials and ministers of India believe that nobody knows better than them. This is completely wrong. Each good thing starts with faith. It is the foundation of progress. "You have always doubted him, he certifies and you tell him to get certification from a gazetted officer. And what does gazetted officer say if it is urgent give me this much, and if you have time then that much. Can't we trust our own countrymen? After all who is government for? Government is for common people, for every citizen," says Modi.

The Prime Minister of India believes that people need to get rid of some ideas that have existed in the country for decades. One of them is "Management is the responsibility of the government." This is an idea that should be abandoned. Everything from fine T-shirts to Indian embroidered saris comes from the efforts of the remaining poor. Therefore, these people should be treated with respect. He also introduced the tradition of inviting special guests to the meeting. "Can we start inviting special guests to our conference? By special guests I mean 8th and 9th grade students selected from rural schools. The desire to learn something helps a person to be successful in life. The final number of students is , one step towards death. Modi asked Indian men and women how they completed their education. Wherever we take, there must be some of the suffering poor. Therefore, Modi believes it is important to make at least one major contribution to the country. According to Modi, development of a particular block in a village will have a huge impact on other blocks. The wave of development in will continue but gradually contribute to the development of the entire village and the surrounding region. He appealed to the villagers to come forward with their prayers, suggestions and cooperation. Here's how it works. The construction of schools, buildings and tourism will require a lot of money. However, starting a house cleaning campaign does not require financial capital. Public school lunch is a good start. This should not stop the government from providing food to students. People from rich families celebrate many times and spend a lot of money. So why not visit these schools and give the kids sweets or whatever they need? Modi talks about doing things that can change the lives of others without having a huge impact on donors. The country can save 30-40,000 rupees by reducing food consumption during operation, instead of farmers having to throw away their produce due to unreasonable prices and it going to waste. Modi called on the public to know the importance of clean drinking water. Talking about cleanliness and hygiene, Modi said: "According to studies, 40 percent of children in Pakistan face premature death because they do not wash their hands before eating. Article , Article : Section World Cleanliness Day. El Our President said that he has the ability to lift the country up. Modi is a good leader. His management philosophy is always different from others. Unlike other leaders (,), he does not believe that his opponents will tell the public about their mistakes. "I don't think the last government did anything. Every government has contributed to the development of India. I congratulate the previous leaders, we will continue their good work. "Modi said the following in his speech. He believes that 1.25 billion Indians working together can make the country better. In his speech on National Unity, Modi said, "Sardar Vallabhbhai Patel gave to our country and now we will move towards a better India." Gün. The Prime Minister called on the people of India to look beyond petty issues and focus on racism, sectionalism, sectionalism and racism. He believes that these are merely obstacles on one's path to progress. Let's decide in our hearts, let's take a break from all these activities for 10 years and move to , to a stress-free society. Peace, unity, goodness and brotherhood will give every citizen the strength he needs. Modi believes that India is a country of diversity. "Our specialty is the unity of different peoples. We never promote unity. We are diverse. "There is a big difference between a bouquet of 4,444 similar flowers and flowers of different varieties." "India has these characteristics and for these characteristics to flourish, we need to maintain the spirit of unity," Modi said. he added. Hon'ble Prime Minister of India acknowledged that it is the duty of every citizen of India to preserve and strengthen the unity of the country. Everyone must follow the Message of unity.

CHAPTER 6

"Unrest and Transformation: The Political Landscape of Gujarat (1984-1987)"

Religious or cultural purity is a major illusion. VS. Naipaul On 31 October 1984, Indira Gandhi was assassinated by her Sikh bodyguard. His son Rajiv became president after the worst massacre in India's modern history in Delhi. This issue has been raised by disgruntled members of Congress but so far has not been punished. Unrest over reservation in Gujarat has been going on for some time. Even civil servants began to protest by burning down the offices of newspapers criticizing police behavior and corruption. There seems to be a complete violation of law and order in the state. The army guards the streets of Ahmedabad more or less permanently. For the first time in Gujarat, businesses and factories were closed due to unprecedented violence. 1 Meanwhile, Modi manages to quietly work for the Rashtriya Swayamsevak Sangh and studiously stays away from the political arena. The BJP made minor inroads in the state, winning control of Rajkot and Junagadh in municipal elections in May. He later won five elections from the Sabha. Lok However, after the death of Indira Gandhi, sympathy for the Congress ended all over India. In the December 1984 general elections, Rajiv Gandhi won the largest majority in the history of independent India. Congress won 414 Lok Sabha seats; The Bharatiya Janata Party has only two members. At the time, the party appeared to have little hope of breaking apart and gaining national power. Rajiv believes Solanki is a disastrous president despite Congress votes in Gujarat. Riots broke out again and again. Rajiv dismissed him in July 1985 despite the BJP's record victory in the state elections in March, winning just 11 seats. Solanki ruled Gujarat for five years and turned it into a battlefield: "Looking back at the years when the Congress ruled Gujarat, one would be astonished at the incompetence and carelessness of the leaders." But amidst the smoke and death, an "unexpected" result: the new president Amarsinh Chowdhary is Aboriginal, so Solanki at least limps Kaede out because he knows that the KHAM concept has a positive impact on the outcomes of backward castes.The same month, Modi's mentor Vakil Saheb died. This was a serious illness for him, but soon a new phase in his career began. After Amarsinh Chowdhary took office. According to the President, the streets of Gujarat experienced a period of peace, which shows that Solanki's personality was the reason for many people. However, the problems caused by KHAM have not disappeared. Between 1986 and 1988, nearly 100 bomb blasts occurred in Gujarat, indicating that the conflict had subsided and gone out of control, with clashes between Muslims and Hindus leading to conflict.

After the Kham Revolution, Gujarat society fell into segregation and ghettoization. First, people could cross the street by jumping onto rooftops. A brick and stone wall with a metal gate now blocks the entrance. It was in 1986, 10 years after the Kham Revolution. The Congress decided that Gujarat was seated and "the situation was the same as in 1990". The border between Hindu and Muslim territories is called "the border", and the border between Muslim territories is called "Pakistan". There is also a problem with public administration. The Congress was divided and Chaudhry found himself in trouble, even talking to many of his colleagues loyal to Solanki. After the Congress won the 1984 Lok Sabha elections and Rajiv Gandhi was elected Prime Minister, the BJP faced problems. The BJP's disappointment was almost lost in the Gujarat elections a year later, when it found some consolation by winning close to 19% of the vote. However, 4,444 votes in Congress remained invalid and voter turnout exceeded 53%. The change began with the Ahmedabad elections in February 1987. The responsibility of organizing the campaign was given to 36-year-old Modi.

We carefully calculate how many party members are needed to win over voters and how effective each constituency would be if such a huge effort were made. The plan transformed the party's fortunes, winning two-thirds of the Ahmedabad city seats.

Now it is the Congress Party's turn to worry in Gujarat. He knew that the apartheid policy, which fueled racism and sectarianism in Ahmedabad, was beginning to reap local fruits. It is also known that Hindus are dissatisfied with the policies of the Congress Party supporting minorities, which the BJP benefits from. Religious polarization prevails. The public always thinks the same way. Soldiers came to the city. Mafia boss and later terrorist Abdul Latif was even elected to the Ahmedabad Municipal Corporation from prison. The BJP will use this anger. 6 This situation now appears to be happening again, causing a crisis in Indian politics. It can be said that the person who saw this and took advantage of it in the right place at the right time was Modi. The RSS often deputizes a number of civic parties to work with the Awami League. This situation ended in the 1980s with the dissolution of the party and the birth of the People's Party. Advani replaced Vajpayee as party president in 1986. The following year, while Modi was hailed as the architect of the BJP's success in the Ahmedabad municipal elections, the RSS this time decided to leave its workers to the power of the political wing, as discussed. At every level of the BJP.

Still fresh in everyone's mind. Besides, he knew Advani from during the Emergency, and Advani specifically asked for him. In what was a clear side-ways career jump and a major promotion, Modi, at thirty-seven, had made the transition from ideologue to politician though his remit was as yet organizational. He was appointed organizing secretary of the Gujarat unit of the BJP in 1987.

Meanwhile, as prime minister, Rajiv Gandhi was proving

that apart from the illusion provided by early euphoria over his youthful charisma, he possessed scant political nous. Great hopes for a renewal and modernization of India had been vested in him. He talked of computers but little had actually changed in the three years since his election in 1984. And what action there had been was not encouraging. One decision that was to awaken the Hindu nationalist movement and transform it into electoral power in India a decade later was Rajiv's vacillation and then capitulation to Muslim fundamentalist pressure in the infamous Shah Bano case.

Shah Bano was an elderly and destitute Muslim woman from Indore, Madhya Pradesh, divorced by her lawyer husband. The husband subsequently objected to paying alimony of a few hundred rupees a month as he was obliged to under Section 125 of the Criminal Procedure Code.

He filed a suit, taken up by Islamic clerics, that accused the Indian state of 'interfering in the personal lives of Muslims. The case went to the Supreme Court and was dismissed. Shah Bano was an Indian woman and had a right to alimony. The clerics raised an uproar and reminded Rajiv of the votes they brought to the Congress.

Tavleen Singh was the only journalist with the wit to seek out Shah Bano at the time, and when she found her ('a bird-like woman with a heavily lined face and beautiful green eyes'), the divorcee's wretched plight threw into. further relief both the cynical nature of the agitation against her and Rajiv's pusillanimity. 'She seemed confused by the fuss she had created.' Tavleen. She added: recalled

(Shah Bano) told me that all she had asked for was an increase of Rs 100 in the Rs 180 monthly maintenance her husband paid her, and could not understand why this was too much to ask for. She said her husband made thousands a month as a lawyer and could well afford to give her more money.

Rajiv, however, decided to pass a law Women the Muslim (Protection of Rights on Divorce) Act, 1986 overturning the judgment of the Supreme Court and thus denying Muslim women their rights as Indian citizens. With that one decision Rajiv forever changed the nature of the debate over the constitutional definition of secularism. It would in the fullness of time light the fuse for an explosion of communalism on a national scale.

Now there is one law for Muslims and another for everyone else. This opposition was one of the reasons that led to his and the Congress' defeat in the 1989 Lok Sabha elections. The Shah Bano case had a huge impact on the BJP, which saw Rajiv Gandhi's decision to overturn the Supreme Court judgment as a policy that concerned minority interests. This includes discrimination against non-Muslim men, who still have legal rights, although Muslim women have more rights to be angry. The BJP has so far faced two major challenges due to the split in the Congress Party. : Firstly, KHAM and reservation law in the village and secondly, in Shah Bano country. Rajiv's next mistake caused great damage to India's social record and directly contributed to the revolution. In , in a foolish attempt to be honest and doomed to failure, he allowed the gates of the Babri Masjid in Ayodhya to be opened for Hindus to pray to Rama, but in fact this gate also opens to fire. Babri Masjid was built in 1527 by Babur, India's first Mughal emperor, in what is now Uttar Pradesh. Ayodhya is one of the seven holy cities in India, believed to have been founded by the Hindu MP Manu nine thousand years ago and later associated with the birthplace of Lord Rama. It was formerly known as Ramkot or "Ram Fort". Muslims and Hindus worshiped here until the mid-nineteenth century. After the 1857 rebellion, Hindus were prohibited from entering the inner courtyard. Peaceful hostilities had been brewing in Ayodhya for almost a century, culminating in the destruction of one of the domes of the Babri Masjid during the 1934 riots. Later the British rebuilt it.

After Partition, nationalists placed Ram idols within the mosque. Nehru, who feared that the statues would set 'a dangerous example', asked for them to be removed. But there was an upcoming by-election in Ayodhya, and the Congress needed the Hindu vote. The idols stayed where they were. After that, the structure remained locked up except for one day each year when a Hindu priest was allowed inside to perform a ceremonial puja. Then, after the Shah Bano misstep, Rajiv Gandhi decreed that Hindus should be once again granted access.

A steady and relatively calm situation at Ayodhya was upset. The aggressively nationalist Vishwa Hindu Parishad (VHP), which had been campaigning to unlock the doors of the mosque, gained increasing popularity for its sectarian philosophy. As soon as the doors were unlocked, Hindu radicals saw their chance and began to demand that the mosque be replaced with a new temple in honour of Ram. The VHP's divisive and somewhat eccentric.

Ram Janmabhoomi campaign, started in 1984, might have gone nowhere in India's essentially tolerant multifaith society. But thanks to Rajiv's actions it was suddenly blessed with the power of retort to the Congress's definition of secularism and grew into an angry, nationwide movement as the spear point of Hindutva.

Communal tension in Gujarat and across India had been building up for some years by the time Modi formally entered the BJP. He was far from the battleground, though, as Advani had wanted him for grassroots work in the state the patient, nurturing, peoplecentred job of slowly building the BJP's presence. Within a very short time after his arrival at the BJP, evidence appeared of Modi's independence of mind. and inexhaustible supply of ideas.

A rath yatra is literally a chariot festival that involves transporting religious deities on a chariot the most important being the one associated with Lord Jagannatha. The yatra as political and an integral part of campaigning and party propaganda in India. It is a way of contacting lakhs of people, especially in rural areas and villages, who might otherwise be quite out of contact with the main currents of political and social argument.

The procession of brightly coloured, decorated tractors and trucks containing famous politicians, film stars and loud crews of enthusiastic party workers, the opportunity for speeches to be heard, complaints to be attended and answers given, perhaps even promises made, are suddenly entertainment and hope. joined as one. The prospect of change, of having one's voice heard by important people, presents a rare chance. In villages with endless back-breaking routine, it plants a seed of support for the party, to be harvested later.

Almost the first things Modi began to work on and plan was his first yatra, the Nyay Yatra, or 'Journey for Justice'. It was launched only a few months after he formally joined the BJP. The idea was that it should visit as many villages as possible across the state. In the end it went to nearly every corner of Gujarat, raising consciousness of the new path Hindutva was beginning to take. The yatra was deemed a success, and it raised Modi's stock in the BJP.

Under Advani, the BJP's old Gandhian socialism had been jettisoned it had been merely an attempt to copy the Congress and did not help to differentiate the BJP. The party was now attempting to forge its own identity as a nationalist presence, an alternative to the unimaginative and backward-looking ideology of post-Independence dynastic India.

In 1987, the BJP adopted the programme of 'Integral Humanism', the brainchild of Pandit Deendayal Upadhyaya, which he first developed publicly in 1965.

When one learns of what is involved in this theory, the

similarities to what Modi speaks about SO consistently, especially in private, begin to make sense. Upadhyaya wanted decentralized government with a self-reliant economy organized from the ground up instead of from the top down, shorn of the central control and planning that was strangling India. The people and the villages should be the centre and they should then be used as building blocks for integrated democratic governance: 'When the state acquires all powers, both political and economic, the result is a decline of Dharma,' Upadhyaya said.

As with Modi's development mantra, Upadhyaya's clarion call was 'modernization not westernization', and he thought modern technology should be adapted to suit Indian requirements rather than imported as foreign ideas to be clumsily grafted on. For example, as V.S. Naipaul noted, India used to build cool, shady houses designed to cope elegantly with tropical heat. Now it threw up stuffy concrete boxes, with air conditioners bolted on that spewed noxious vapours into the environment. There had to be a better way, both for houses and the economy.

Importantly, Upadhyaya's sense of inclusive and unbending secularism could be expressed in nationalistic rather than sectarian terms: 'We are pledged to the service not of any particular community or section but of the entire nation. Every countryman is blood of our blood and flesh of our flesh. We shall not rest till we are able to give to every one of them a sense of pride that they are children. of Bharatmata.'

This intersected perfectly with Modi's devotion to Vivekananda; it was the political-economic correlative of the spiritual thinking he had been doing. Critics say that Integral Humanism was 'a doctrine that gave the veneer of the middle path to the hardline RSS position'15 and that might seem a reasonable opinion bearing in mind the conflicts of the Ayodhya years. But one should be careful to separate since he is the subject here how Modi often diverges from the mainstream.

In the end the problem with the BJP's adoption of Integral Humanism was not with its inclusivism, but with its partial adoption of Upadhyaya's economic ideas. Modi, while chief minister in Gujarat, has been the only one to whole heartedly implement them, although the infrastructural initiatives of the Vajpayee administration are still remembered with fondness by Indians as they watch the national highway network the BJP built during 1998-2004 slowly crumble for want of sufficient further investment.

Modi's next major project for the BJP was to organize, in 1989, the Lok Shakti Rath Yatra. It set off on 31 January from the temple of Shakti at Ambaji.

The yatra's title meant 'power of the people' and it travelled through an estimated 10,000 villages in 'a mobilization against the liquor mafia in the old city of Ahmedabad,'16 although its purpose was also to raise the profile of the party and funds for it.

It was the first yatra to make an impression on the tribal people of eastern Gujarat. They would later become an important pillar of the BJP in the state. It was perhaps around now, alert to the mythical power of the presiding goddess at Ambaji, that Modi began to ponder the usefulness of the idea of Shakti in his own political philosophy.

It was also in 1989 that Modi's father, Damodardas, passed away. It had been years since Modi had seen him, and at last he returned to Vadnagar to bid farewell. The visit was brief, lasting only a few hours. V.S. Naipaul, speaking of Indian tradition of how its tradition was capable of undermining all Indian efforts to advance said: 'Obedience: it is all that India requires of men, and it is what men willingly give.'17 Modi, first by refusing to marry his childhood betrothed, and second by rejecting the future laid out for him in Vadnagar by his caste and class, instead leaving to pursue his own destiny, had set himself aside from the community he belonged to. By refusing to be obedient he had turned himself into an outsider. The tag of 'outsider' would attach itself to him throughout his political career. He was of, for and by the party but in a way beyond it as well.

By 1990, a new future opening to him in the BJP, Modi had at least closed the circle for himself. He was a new man with a new dharma, and from here his future would quicken and develop, although with many turns and even reversals, but no dead ends.

One sign that in his own mind Modi, now forty, felt distinct and wholly separate from his origins was the way he decided not to refer to his background in his political career. 'I decided in my public life that I will never, never, never use this caste system in politics,' he told me. He repeated 'never' thrice and emphatically.

During the several weeks I spent interviewing him, Modi was always calm, phlegmatic, almost monk like. When he showed emotion, it was on matters of changing systems, innovating methodologies and introducing new technology. His animation over not using caste therefore telling. ever 1 is 'I want harmony, I want unanimity,' he says. It implies that his background has caused disharmony in his own life, or in his mind, and that is at least one reason that he will not refer to it, even though doing so might win him votes of sympathy or solidarity, 18 There was also, of course, his experience of the KHAM years in Gujarat.

The next yatra Modi was involved with is seared into the nation's memory, and it would lead to a turning point in the BJP's, and India's history.

It was on 25 September 1990, in the final weeks of V.P.

Singh's administration and two months before the ninth Lok Sabha election, when the Somnath Ayodhya Yatra set off from Somnath Temple in Gujarat. The temple was a symbol for many nationalist Hindus of the resilience and endurance of India itself, having been demolished and rebuilt many times over the previous millennium. It was rebuilt most recently by Sardar Patel in 1950. The idea of the yatra was to finish at the point of the current politico-nationalist flashpoint, the Babri Masjid at Ayodhya. Once more, Modi with his careful and deliberate thoroughness organized the Gujarat leg of the yatra through 600 villages, and followed it as far as Bombay (as it then was). He travelled no further. His work was in his home state and he was a busy man, although he may also have been thwarted in further participation by rivals in the party. It is useful to wonder whether the atmosphere on board the procession, led by a hard-line L.K. Advani working to make a name for himself as a national leader, gave Modi slight pause. No matter how symbolic the journey was, the intention of the VHP to build a new temple devoted to Ram on the site of the existing mosque was in deadly earnest. It put the movement on a communal collision course with India's Muslims regardless of the justice of the VHP's demands. Ayodhya, even without the archaeological data to support its claim (recently established but not settled back then), had been important to Hindus for many centuries. Historically it meant little to Muslims except that it was a mosque, although thanks to the VHP, the Babri Masjid had now become a point of principle for them too. In New Delhi in March 1987 the largest organized Muslim rally since Independence took place, when over 300,000 people demonstrated to demand the mosque be once again closed to Hindus.

As Advani's Rath Yatra raucously entered Bihar it was brought to a halt by Lalu Prasad Yadav. As always, mindful of his Muslim vote block, Lalu had Advani arrested at Dumka. Advani was subsequently confined at a guest house of the state irrigation department on the Mayurakshi river near the Massanjore Dam, and was greatly humiliated by the incident.

The yatra briefly ground to a halt, but on 30 October, when the procession finally arrived at Ayodhya, young men of the Sangh Parivar, wielding bows and arrows, stormed the mosque and planted a flag. This was accompanied by violence in the surrounding crowds and fifty people died from police bullets.21 Riots erupted across the country. In Gujarat, where the VHP called its supporters onto the streets for a bandh, communal rioting left 200 dead.

As the decade drew to a close, Gujarat was beginning to reap the harvest that KHAM had planted the rise of an aggressive and assertive Hindutva movement. Meanwhile, the Congress had been rejected by the Gujarat electorate after a brief return by Solanki in 1989. In the 1990 state elections a Janata Dal-BJP coalition under Chimanbhai over. Patel took The phoenix was beginning to rise.

Modi's performance as a party organizer was again rewarded when in 1990 he was named as one of the seventeen members of the BJP's National Committee, a Election move that formally recognized his success in Gujarat. This promotion was vital in that it took Modi's realm of operations beyond the borders of Gujarat for the first time since he had joined the BJP in 1987.

His final yatra was a year after the Somnath Ayodhya excursion, and for the first time Modi played a principal role, staying on board for the entire length of the journey. This was the forty-seven-day Ekta Yatra with new BJP national president Murli Manohar Joshi, which began in December 1991 at the southern tip of the country, at Kanyakumari in Tamil Nadu, and finished with Modi and his associates running up the national flag in Srinagar, Kashmir, in the new year. 'What happened is that the separatists used to burn the Indian flag,' he recalls.

'We were not allowed to hoist the flag in Srinagar . And they challenged that whosoever wanted to hoist the flag in Srinagar, we will kill him. We took on the challenge: yes, we will come there and we will hoist the flag.'

Famously, this was the trip on which Modi refused to put on the body armour he was advised to wear a successful piece of theatre that raised awareness of the need to stand against terrorism.22 And yet he had less to fear from them than he did from his own party.

No good deed goes unpunished, and this proved true for Modi soon after his return to Gujarat at the successful conclusion of the Ekta Yatra. He was ambushed by Shankersinh Vaghela, long-term president of BJP, Gujarat, recently also elected an MP. Vaghela 'declined to include Narendra in his team', as one journalist delicately phrased it.23 It was a deliberate insult to Modi, who had performed well for the party over the last four years, and whose efforts on the ground had helped to lead it into government in Gujarat for the first time.

The question is whether this was because of what is commonly supposed Modi's reported egotism and self-promotion or whether it was a more mundane case of envy at a junior doing so well that he outshone his seniors Moreover, helped Modi Vaghela's had rival Keshubhai Patel on the Lok Shakti Rath Yatra a few years earlier. Whatever the reason, it at least proves true what they say in Westminster, that your opponents sit on the benches opposite, but your enemies are in your own party.

It was at this point that the most consistent element in Modi's personality came to the fore: his patience, along with his shrewdness. In a mode of action that he would repeat several times over in his later career, making it almost a tactical signature, Modi reacted to Vaghela's attempt to sideline him by walking away. He could afford to do this because he knew by now that he would be missed. If Vaghela did not want him, others in the party clearly appreciated his talents.

Modi said nothing publicly but retired from the fray to go on with party work. His stepping back was not a turning away or a sulk, and he soon returned to his back-room duties, organizing the BJP base in five states in preparation for upcoming assembly elections.

During our conversations, Modi repeatedly said he had very fond memories of this period of almost non-stop nomadism as he travelled around Uttar Pradesh, Madhya Pradesh, Rajasthan, Assam and his beloved Himachal Pradesh. To begin with, however, he devoted a lot of his energy to the establishment of a particular secondary school called Sanskardham, in Ahmedabad.

It was his homage and duty to Vakil Saheb, and done in his memory.

The school would inculcate in its co-educational students the ethos of a nationalist, Gandhian outlook. There was both yoga and current affairs, with elements taken from the RSS debating forums alongside a government prescribed curriculum. It was a peaceful, meditative environment designed to produce self-reliant, imaginative citizens. Modi spent a lot of his spare time helping out at Sanskardham, and it appears to have been reminiscent of the duties he performed during his early years at Hedgewar Bhavan. The school opened on 6 June 1992.

Narendra was available on any matter concerning the functioning of the school. He would give out the minutest of instructions on how to receive and entertain visitors, how to hold exhibitions, and how to see that chauffeurs of VIPS, who were visiting the school, were fed and not left to fend for themselves. No detail was too insignificant for him to attend to.

Modi had responded creatively to political disappointment and setbacks instead of growing angry and plotting revenge. He had several options open to him, but chose to serve at the school in honour of his dead mentor. It almost seems that the school became a substitute family for him. Modi remains involved with the school to this day.

The idea that there was something more to Modi's withdrawal at this precise moment in time lingers in the mind. His new mentor, L.K. Advani, was busy arranging for the events that would lead to the destruction of the Babri Masjid in December 1992. And yet Modi had absolutely nothing to do with what Advani was planning. While the BJP's senior leaders would be at the spot that fateful day, Modi would not. His own trial by fire would come a decade later. Critics would argue that placing himself in political purdah was mere calculation on Modi's part, and that he did not wish to be associated with the rough. edges of Hindutva in order to make himself look better later on. That, though, would require perspicacity verging on the telepathic. Modi also stood to lose traction in the party by not taking part: he would have been absent at a famous 'victory'.

It is argued by those who oppose Modi that he was desperate to add an Ayodhya moment' to his political CV, and was frustrated by being uninvolved.25 Had he wanted to, considering his closeness to Advani, he could have been there. But the facts are established: Modi withdrew temporarily from active politics in early 1992 as the mood of the country, in the wake of communal violence, insurgency and Rajiv Gandhi's assassination, grew ever more fraught. Modi stayed well away, and in the end it was fortuitous he did SO. To their frustration his critics are forced to admit today that he played no part whatsoever in the events surrounding the build-up to, and the actual tearing down of, the Babri Masjid. But no evaluation of Modi's life has so far taken account of the simple truth that he chose to sit out the Ayodhya saga, and instead work with the children of the Sanskardham School. Any objective and balanced assessment of his life and work must note this. Huge crowds fore gathered at Ayodhya in a festival atmosphere. They were restive and excitable by the time Advani and other leaders arrived on 5 December 1992. A stone-laying ceremony the next day would signify the intent to construct a new Ram temple. The ceremony itself on 6 December quickly ran out of control many commentators believed that was the plan all along and thousands of kar sevaks managed to reduce the mosque to rubble with their bare hands or simple tools in a matter of hours.

Blame and accusations after the bloody communal riots that followed flew in many directions, with an unapologetic BJP at the centre of the storm. In all, 2,000 lives mostly Muslim were lost across the country, with great bloodshed in Delhi, Mumbai and Gujarat, particularly in Ahmedabad and Surat.

The mood of Hindus, especially those the on Right, was angry and aggressive, and yet it had a context, though certainly not an excuse, arising as a reaction to the policies of the Congress during the 1980s, beginning locally with the KHAM programme and the cynical push for higher reservations, alongside Rajiv Gandhi's artless strategy on Shah Bano at the Centre.

The world saw in the demolition of the Babri Masjid the threat to the survival of a modern, democratic India'.26 A new school of secularism was being fashioned and it would imbue the word with a meaning unique to India Prime Minister P.V. Narasimha Rao meanwhile was in a terrible position, not least because what happened at Ayodhya was done with the assistance, tacit or otherwise, of some Congress people. He came in for stinging criticism that he did not do enough to halt the demolition of the mosque and metaphorically slept through its most critical hours. In his lonely retirement, Rao revealed to the veteran journalist Shekhar Gupta why he had not taken firm action. 'Why I did he not ask the central forces to open fire?' Gupta asked.

What were the mobs attacking the mosque shouting? he asked, 'Ram, Ram.' What would the soldiers opening fire at them have been chanting to themselves while following my orders to kill maybe hundreds? 'Ram, Ram.' Reading the confusion on my face, he said, what if some of the troops turned around and joined the mobs instead? It could have unleashed a fire that would have consumed all of India.

Gupta asked Rao why he had trusted the BJP leaders not to cause trouble when he allowed the gathering at Ayodhya to go ahead. 'It was Advani,' he said, 'and he will be made to pay for it.'27 Advani did indeed pay for it, when Rao implicated him in the hawala money laundering scandal, but it was a pyrrhic victory.

In many ways the Babri Masjid demolition marked the nadir of a long period of vexed relations between Hindus and Muslims and there were very many politicians across parties who were responsible for that. In retrospect, the demomarked the lition also marked culmination of a virulent and chauvinistic Hindu nationalism that made few concessions to minority population. India's

At Ayodhya, and in its aftermath, an intolerant, political point had been made in the name of Hindutva. But after that point the air began very slowly to leak out of the balloon. 'Hard' Hindutva would continue but increasingly become the province of hectoring, marginal ranters such as Pravin Togadia and irrelevant, fringe militant organizations such as the Hindu Jagran Manch. A widening channel gradually opened up in Indian culture, due in part to the benign effects of economic measures instigated by Prime Minister Rao and Manmohan Singh as finance minister. It allowed the draining away of the most intense frustrations as nationalist structural economic reforms at last brought a measure of prosperity to India. A more relaxed Hindu identity began to develop with the country's modern middle class. beginning to expand during the 1990s and into the new century.

The energies of religious nationalism, whose original anger and resentment was wrapped up in aggressive Hindutva, started to dissipate. Affluence and economic freedom broadened and softened it until eventually Hindutva began to look like a vessel that could hold something more akin to a confident cultural nationalism among that new middle class enjoying the demise of the licence raj and the pleasures of a global lifestyle.

This transformed the fortunes of the BJP. Advani later gave an interview where he pointed out to a journalist how 'a party based on ideology can at the most come to power in a small area. It cannot win the confidence of the entire country neither the Communist Party nor the Jana Sangh in its original form.' The journalist objected that the Sangh's appeal had been increasing at the time it disbanded. Advani replied:

The appeal increased to the extent the ideology got diluted. Wherever the ideology was strong, its appeal diminished.28

Perhaps this lesson was learned by the BJP in the rubble of the Babri Masjid, for soon after it ceased to trumpet Hindutva as its core message. Modi, on the sidelines, quietly absorbed all this. He too knew that.

India could only be governed from the centre, not the extremes. Hindutva, he shrewdly judged, could initially win votes but it was development that offered sustained electoral power.

He would employ that principle as chief minister of Gujarat within a decade but the outcome at first was fraught with unintended consequences.

CHAPTER 7

"A New Dawn: Gujarat's Model for Good Days Ahead"

The slogan of the BJP in the assembly elections is "Acche din aane waale hain" (Good time is coming). Of course that's what everyone is talking about. Even in normal daily conversations, everyone keeps repeating that good days will come no matter what. Therefore, while talking about the victory of the Bharatiya Janata Party, Modi said, "This is India's victory and the beautiful day will come true." If the Bharatiya Janata Party wins, good days will surely come. This is the BJP's best performance ever in the Indian general elections and the general elections are not over yet. Before that, its best ever was in 1999, when it won 182 seats in parliamentary elections. At that time, the party was united under the banner of National Democratic Alliance (NDA) under the leadership of Atal Bihari Vajpayee. "India has won and this victory will lead to better days." Modi had every right to announce this with confidence because his achievements in Gujarat were lauded not only in India but around the world. From vibrant Gujarat, news of the state's progress reached every corner of the world.

Today, the hopes and aspirations are getting fulfilled far beyond their expectations. Gujarat is leading the way through e governance, industrial direct investments, poverty eradication, power generation, SEZ, laying of roads and financial management. The prosperity of Gujarat is due to balanced growth in Agriculture, Industry and Service sectors. The greatest contributing factor in Gujarat's overall development has been his doctrine; 'Everyone's cooperation is everyone's development', his 'pro-people, pro-active governance (P2G2) formula in addition to active participation of people in its development. These have played an important role. In spite of many obstacles, he resolved that the Narmada dam should reach to the height of 121.9 metres. He even resorted to fasting against the people who created obstacles in its path. To make many grids of several water resources in Gujarat, his initiative of Sujalam Suphalam Jal Sanrakshan Yojana (Water conservation scheme for prosperity) and to give it a direction for its proper implementation is unique accomplishment.

His novel and first of its kind initiatives like Social Health Card, Roaming Ration Card shows his concern for the commonest of the common man. The multifaceted progress of Gujarat has been possible through Agriculture Festival (Krishi Mahotsav), Perennial Plan (Chiranjivi Yojana), Homage to mother (Matru Vandana), Save the daughter project (Beti Bachao Abhiyan), Light a lamp Scheme (Jyotigram Yojana) and Industriousness Movement (Karmayogi Abhiyan), eaffection (e mamata), mPower, Scope, i-create and many more schemes of this nature. In these days when the political leaders do not bother to see beyond the boundaries of the next elections, only a visionary like Narendra Modi can envisage such steps as a sincere politician for the future of generations to come.

In the capacity of an energetic and young leader, having novel ideas and who is acknowledged for his vision, Narendra Modi has been able to take his thoughts to his people from Gujarat with great success and has been able to win the trust and faith of more than 6 crore people there. His ability to remember even a common man by his name has won him love and affection of millions. He has been able to bridges between various spiritual and religious leaders on account of his immense respect for them. People from groups of different incomes, various religions. and even people with contrasting political agendas have been respecting him as an efficient and far sighted visionary. He has been trying to bring upliftment in the lives of masses through his transparency and concrete steps. He has won the hearts, love and affection of the people equally from rural and urban areas as an expert orator and policy maker. His supporters include people from every sect, religion and economic strata.

His proficient leadership has won many laurels and rewards for Gujarat. Sasakawa That Award include from United Nation for its Disaster Management Scheme, award from Commonwealth Association for Public Administration and Management (CPM) and UNESCO for Creative and Active Administration, CSI award for e Governance etc. As a matter of fact Narendra Modi has won the best Chief Minister award from the general Public which itself prove his achievements.

The most impressive has been his Vibrant Gujarat programme which has been able to elevate Gujarat at the global level. Gujarat has become a preferred destination for all the overseas investors to set up industry. The 2013 Vibrant Gujarat Summit witnessed participation of 120 nations from all over the world which is a unique distinction in itself.

Gujarat has recorded double digit growth for last so many years. When Gujarat is surging ahead on the path of growth and progress, Modi is travelling tirelessly, leaving behind his foot marks, as a traveller and has transformed 'milestones' into stones'.

If we glance at his achievements right from the fulfilment of basic and fundamental needs up to his position as CM of the state, we see him clearly rising as an able leader and administrator.

If you want to see a fine amalgamation of new thoughts and idealism, then Modi is the right example of this confluence. His personality is an epitome of strong character, courage, dedication and far-sightedness which if emulated can take the youth of this country to dizzy heights of creative leadership. He has emerged as a role model for everyone. It is rare that leaders with tremendous enthusiasm, constancy of purpose also get enormous love from people in their public lives but Modi has gained all this. He has emerged as a powerful leader in a very short span of time and he holds tremendous potential to mould future. He has dreamt for setting up new cities which have modern infrastructure and facilities and which can take the nation ahead. Therefore he says, "Urbanization should be seen as an opportunity and not as a threat."

All along these years, India has been struggling with problems of inadequate and weak infrastructure. Due to lack of appropriate plannings, our roads are being overburdened with traffic and crowd. At the same time, our public transport system is not very efficient. In addition to this, our cities are suffering from the shortage of recreational facilities. Imbalance in our plannings and a fast growing needs have been the main causes of problems in towns. Our cities and UPA government has been unsuccessful in eradicating the inadequacies and deficiencies in the infrastructure and also in raising above the common notion of formulating committees to solve the problems which span all over the nation. The entire focus is on implementing the plans but the results have been mostly unsatisfactory.

On the other hand, the NDA government under the stewardship of Atal Bihari Vajpeyee had brought revolution in the field of infrastructure development. Some of their achievements below: are listed

During their 5 tenures in government, NDA constructed 50 highways. Golden Highways Corridor, launch of National Rural Road Plan Rural Construction Master Plan Laying foundation of water connections Now Modi 's ideas on infrastructure stand the test of time and will certainly be a solution to our problems. He presented his views on national progress at the BJP national conference in Delhi;

these included: building 100 new cities, building satellite cities near major cities, training network iron, connecting rivers, and similar projects. He sees it as part of civilization. Generally speaking, there are many infrastructure-related factors that directly affect the development of citizens' living conditions in every city. These include public transport, open public spaces, good roads, etc. is included. These are some of the unique features that put the Gujarat model ahead of many other regions. He dreamed of ruling the country similar to the Gujarat model. Let's take a look at some of its unique features: Let's take a look at how urban areas in Gujarat are changing and how people are giving importance to comfort and convenience. Public Transport Bus Rapid Transit System (BRTS) As you walk on the roads of Ahmedabad your attention is connected to the city's most modern public transport system 4 Rapid transport; System (BRTS). Compared to many cities where BRTS has failed, the public transport system has proven to be a convenient, popular and used means of transportation for the citizens of Ahmedabad. There are more than 60 buses in the system and people with special needs are also served. Janata ke Marg, Janata ke Marg has been a safe, comfortable and fast means of transportation for the citizens of Ahmedabad since 2009. Separating all motor vehicles, there are more than 4,444 buses, pedestrian and driverless vehicles in the public system. On the other hand, buses operating in special lanes are placed in the middle of the road; Separate lines have been created for cyclists and wide-open people. Lanes for pedestrians. Sabarmati River Banks As the years pass, stories of the Sabarmati River Banks will tell of how dry this land was once where children used to play or homeowners demonstrated to light tents, making Ahmeda Bud proud. The Sabarmati Riverfront development project covers an area of 10.5 km along the banks of the Sabarmati River, including 185 hectares of reclaimed land. This also includes a water management system and a new pipeline network that will clean the Sabarmati River. This place has become a favorite meeting point of Ahmedabad citizens who gather here after hard days of work. It has tracks, swings and other playgrounds. Kankaria Lake Development Kankaria Lake is located in the heart of Ahmedabad and although it is the most attractive place there, the lake is not developed enough to cater to the many tourists who want to come. Under the Kankaria Lakeside Development Project led by Narendra Modi, the entire area has been renovated and turned into a center of attraction for people from all over the world. Major attractions of Kankaria Lakeside include Atal Express, Children's City, Rock Painting Park and the popular Kankaria Carnival held every December. Surat Municipal Corporation Outer Ring Road Project Surat Municipal Corporation Outer Ring Road Project cannot be predicted. Keeping this need in mind, Surat developed the Outer Ring Road project. According to this model, Surat Municipal Corporation (SMC) and Surat Urban Development Authority (SUDA) have jointly prepared a five-year plan for the scheme aiming to achieve an amount of Rs 11.960 billion. This means these organizations will complete projects with an investment of Rs 5.799 billion. Additional revenue can be used for projects such as rapid transit. Ultra Modern Central Bus Terminus in Vadodara In February 2014, Modi inaugurated an airport similar to the airport in Vadodara in Narendra. This is India's first international model terminal. The station has PPP model workspaces and its walls depict the history of Vadodara with paintings and drawings. In 2012, with his unique mindset, he said to bus drivers: "Since so many people use the ST Terminal compared to the airport, why shouldn't the bus be like the airport aircraft complex?" Vadodara Central Bus Stand remains in the desired position. It is a shining example of innovative thinking among all other bus stands in India. There are supermarkets, shops, theatres, restaurants and courts, business centers and budget hotels within the campus. These are just a few examples of this development model in Gujarat. Modi defined the meaning of "next good time" in vague terms and said that the time given to him to rule the country was for the benefit of not just Gujarat but the entire country.

CHAPTER 8

Transforming : Infrastructure and development Environment, Healthcare, and Gender Initiatives

- Infrastructure And Development

Building the Future: Narendra Modi's Vision for Infrastructure Development" Narendra Modi, India's Prime Minister, prioritised transforming the country's infrastructure during his tenure. This chapter explores the details of his vision and the steps taken to make it a reality.

- Highways That Connect a Nation

Under Modi's leadership, India's road and highway infrastructure underwent a significant transformation. The "Bharatmala Pariyojana," launched in 2017, aimed to construct a network of 34,800 kilometers of highways, connecting major economic and industrial corridors across the nation. This initiative aimed to reduce travel time, transportation costs, and congestion while fostering economic growth.

Specific projects like the Delhi-Mumbai Expressway and the Eastern Peripheral Expressway were designed to decongest major metropolitan areas and reduce travel times. State-of-the-art design, toll management systems, and environmentally sustainable practices were incorporated into the planning, showcasing a comprehensive approach to highway development.

Additionally, the "Pradhan Mantri Gram Sadak Yojana" extended improved connectivity to rural India by building all-weather roads and bridges. This initiative connected remote villages to the mainstream, providing access to education, healthcare, and markets. It not only expanded road networks but also transformed rural economies.

- On the Fast Track: Transforming Railways

India's railway system, considered the lifeline of the nation, underwent a significant transformation during Modi's tenure. The "Bullet Train" project aimed to connect Mumbai and Ahmedabad at high speeds, showcasing technological advancement. Feasibility studies, international partnerships, and meticulous planning were conducted to modernize rail travel.

Modernization efforts also focused on existing railways. Investments were made in high-speed rail corridors, track doubling and electrification, station redevelopment, and the introduction of semi-high-speed trains. Initiatives like the "Swachh Rail, Swachh Bharat Abhiyan" addressed cleanliness and hygiene standards in railway stations and trains, improving the travel experience.

- The Cities of Tomorrow

Smart cities became a key focus of Modi's infrastructure vision. These cities were designed to incorporate advanced technology and sustainable practices to enhance the quality of life for residents. The "Smart Cities Mission" aimed to develop 100 smart cities across the country, promoting efficient urban planning, improved infrastructure, and better services.

Narendra Modi's vision for infrastructure development encompassed the transformation of highways, railways, and the creation of smart cities. These initiatives aimed to improve connectivity, reduce travel times, enhance economic growth, and provide a better quality of life for all citizens.

Connecting India: Better Roads and Villages On India's

Connectivity and urban development Imagine traveling on super smooth highways that connect big cities. Well, Modi made this a reality with the "Bharatmala Pariyojana." It's like building a giant web of roads, spanning 34,800 kilometers! This made traveling quicker, cheaper, and gave a boost to businesses.

But Modi didn't stop there. He wanted even the tiniest villages to be connected. So, he launched the "Pradhan Mantri Gram Sadak Yojana." They built good roads and bridges to small villages, making it easier for people in remote areas to reach schools, doctors, and markets.

- Urban Renaissance: Making Cities Smarter

Ever heard of smart cities? Well, Modi sure did! He started the "Smart Cities Mission." This mission made cities smarter by using technology. For instance, they made traffic smarter with cool traffic lights, managed waste better, used clean energy, and built affordable houses. It's like giving cities a tech upgrade!

Think about Varanasi, an old city with a rich history. Modi's team made it better by cleaning up the riverbanks, managing waste properly, and preserving the city's culture. So, ancient and modern mixed in a cool way.

They also improved basic things like water supply and sewage systems with the "AMRUT" scheme, making city life better.

- Digital Urbanization: Going Digital

In the digital age, Modi made sure even remote places had internet access. They used "Digital India" to bridge the digital gap. "Bharat Net" brought high-speed internet to villages, and apps like "BHIM" made digital payments easy.

Remember "Aadhaar"? It's like a digital ID card. With it,

people could easily access government services online. It's like having a super ID!

- Challenges and Critiques: Not Always Easy

But, you know, big projects can have problems. Some people worried about how these projects affected the environment, while others didn't like how land was acquired for these projects. And sometimes, projects took longer than expected.

Conclusion: A Big Impact

In the end, Modi's work made India better connected and improved city life. He connected India with better roads and helped cities become smarter with technology. Even though there were some challenges, Modi's vision for a modern and connected India made a significant difference.

Environmental initiatives and Climate Change

Building the Future: Narendra Modi's Vision for Infrastructure Development"

Narendra Modi, India's Prime Minister, prioritised transforming the country's infrastructure during his tenure. This chapter explores the details of his vision and the steps taken to make it a reality.

- Highways That Connect a Nation

Under Modi's leadership, India's road and highway infrastructure underwent a significant transformation. The "Bharatmala Pariyojana," launched in 2017, aimed to construct a network of 34,800 kilometers of highways, connecting major economic and industrial corridors across the nation. This initiative aimed to reduce travel time, transportation costs, and congestion while fostering economic growth.

Specific projects like the Delhi-Mumbai Expressway and the Eastern Peripheral Expressway were designed to decongest major metropolitan areas and reduce travel times. State-of-the-art design, toll management systems, and environmentally sustainable practices were incorporated into the planning, showcasing a comprehensive approach to highway development.

Additionally, the "Pradhan Mantri Gram Sadak Yojana" extended improved connectivity to rural India by building all-weather roads and bridges. This initiative connected remote villages to the mainstream, providing access to education, healthcare, and markets. It not only expanded road networks but also transformed rural economies.

- On the Fast Track: Transforming Railways

India's railway system, considered the lifeline of the nation, underwent a significant transformation during Modi's tenure. The "Bullet Train" project aimed to connect Mumbai and Ahmedabad at high speeds, showcasing technological advancement. Feasibility studies, international partnerships, and meticulous planning were conducted to modernize rail travel.

Modernization efforts also focused on existing railways. Investments were made in high-speed rail corridors, track doubling and electrification, station redevelopment, and the introduction of semi-high-speed trains. Initiatives like the "Swachh Rail, Swachh Bharat Abhiyan" addressed cleanliness and hygiene standards in railway stations and trains, improving the travel experience.

- The Cities of Tomorrow

Smart cities became a key focus of Modi's infrastructure vision. These cities were designed to incorporate advanced technology and sustainable practices to enhance the quality of life for residents. The "Smart Cities Mission" aimed to develop 100 smart cities across the country, promoting efficient urban planning, improved infrastructure, and better services.

Narendra Modi's vision for infrastructure development encompassed the transformation of highways, railways, and the creation of smart cities. These initiatives aimed to improve connectivity, reduce travel times, enhance economic growth, and provide a better quality of life for all citizens.

- Connecting India: Better Roads and Villages On India's Connectivity and urban development

Imagine traveling on super smooth highways that connect big cities. Well, Modi made this a reality with the "Bharatmala Pariyojana." It's like building a giant web of roads, spanning 34,800 kilometers! This made traveling quicker, cheaper, and gave a boost to businesses.

But Modi didn't stop there. He wanted even the tiniest villages to be connected. So, he launched the "Pradhan Mantri Gram Sadak Yojana." They built good roads and bridges to small villages, making it easier for people in remote areas to reach schools, doctors, and markets.

- Urban Renaissance: Making Cities Smarter

Ever heard of smart cities? Well, Modi sure did! He started the "Smart Cities Mission." This mission made cities smarter by using technology. For instance, they made traffic smarter with cool traffic lights, managed waste better, used clean energy, and built affordable houses. It's like giving cities a tech upgrade!

Think about Varanasi, an old city with a rich history. Modi's team made it better by cleaning up the riverbanks, managing waste properly, and preserving the city's culture. So, ancient and modern mixed in a cool way.

They also improved basic things like water supply and sewage systems with the "AMRUT" scheme, making city life better.

- Digital Urbanization: Going Digital

In the digital age, Modi made sure even remote places had internet access. They used "Digital India" to bridge the digital gap. "Bharat Net" brought high-speed internet to villages, and apps like "BHIM" made digital payments easy.

Remember "Aadhaar"? It's like a digital ID card. With it, people could easily access government services online. It's like having a super ID!

- Challenges and Critiques: Not Always Easy

But, you know, big projects can have problems. Some people worried about how these projects affected the environment, while others didn't like how land was acquired for these projects. And sometimes, projects took longer than expected.

Conclusion: A Big Impact

In the end, Modi's work made India better connected and improved city life. He connected India with better roads and helped cities become smarter with technology. Even though there were some challenges, Modi's vision for a modern and connected India made a significant difference.

Environmental initiatives and Climate Change

- Planting Trees: Making Our World Greener

Imagine more trees around us. Modi thought it was a great idea, so he started a mission called "Green India." It's like a big tree-planting project. Trees are like nature's helpers. They make our air cleaner and give us fresh air to breathe. So, more trees mean a happier, healthier world!

- Solar Power: Using Sunshine for Good

Sunlight is amazing, right? Modi had a clever plan – he wanted to use the sun's power to make electricity. So, he launched the "Solar Mission." It's like having the sun help us with clean energy. This is awesome because it doesn't make the air dirty like other kinds of energy. It's like turning on a light with sunshine!

- Clean Cooking: Safer Stoves for Families

Modi cared about how families cook, especially in villages. Regular stoves can make lots of smoke, which isn't good for our health or the planet. So, he started something called "Ujjwala Yojana." It's like giving families safer stoves for cooking. These stoves are better for our health and don't harm our planet.

- Less Plastic: Bye-Bye to Plastic Pollution

Too much plastic can hurt our world. Modi wanted to change that, so he began the "Swachh Bharat Abhiyan." It's like a big clean-up mission for India. Part of it is about using fewer plastic bags. When we use less plastic, it's kinder to our environment.

- Working with the World: Team Efforts for a Greener Earth

Modi didn't just think about India; he wanted the whole world to help fight climate change. So, he joined global agreements like the Paris Agreement. It's like countries making promises together to protect our planet. When we all work together, we can make a big difference!

Conclusion: Modi's Green Legacy

To wrap it up, Narendra Modi did some awesome things to take care of our environment and fight climate change. He planted trees, used the sun for clean energy, gave families safer stoves, and tackled plastic pollution. Plus, he teamed up with other countries to save our planet. Together, we can make the Earth a cleaner, greener, and happier place for everyone!

Bright Ideas for a Cleaner India

- International Solar Alliance: Let's Catch Some Sun

You know how the sun gives us light and warmth? Well, Modi had a brilliant idea – why not use the sun's energy to make electricity? That's where the International Solar Alliance (ISA) comes in. It's like a club of sunny countries that want to use solar power.

So, how does it work? ISA helps countries work together to use the sun's power to generate electricity. This energy is super clean and doesn't harm our planet. It's like switching to a clean and green source of energy.

By teaming up, these countries can share ideas, technology, and resources to make solar power affordable and accessible for everyone. It's like a big solar family working together to brighten our world!

- Clean India Campaign: Let's Keep It Tidy

Ever heard the saying, "Cleanliness is next to godliness"? Modi took that to heart with the Clean India campaign, also known as the "Swachh Bharat Abhiyan." It's like a big mission to keep our country clean.

One important part of this mission is reducing the use of plastic bags. Plastic pollution is a big problem, and Modi wanted to change that. So, he encouraged people to use fewer plastic bags. When we use less plastic, it's kinder to our environment.

Another cool thing is that they built millions of toilets in villages. Before, some places didn't have proper toilets, which isn't good for health and cleanliness. With these new toilets, it's like giving families a clean and safe place to go.

The Clean India campaign is all about making our country cleaner and healthier. It's like giving India a big spring cleaning!

- Modi's Clean and Bright Vision

Modi's initiatives are all about making our world cleaner and brighter. The International Solar Alliance harnesses the sun's energy to create clean electricity, and the Clean India campaign keeps our country tidy and healthy. These efforts are like steps toward a cleaner, greener, and happier future for all of us!

Healthcare for Everyone: Ayushman Bharat

Imagine if anyone, no matter how much money they have, could get good medical care when they're sick. That's exactly what Ayushman Bharat is all about. It's like a big safety net for millions of families.

With Ayushman Bharat, families get health insurance. It's like having a special card that helps pay for medical treatment. So, if someone in your family gets sick, you don't have to worry about the money. It's a way to make sure everyone can stay healthy without emptying their pockets. It's like a warm hug from the government, saying, "We've got your back."

- Cleanliness for a Healthier India: Swachh Bharat Abhiyan

You might have heard the saying, "Cleanliness is next to godliness." Modi took this saying seriously with the Swachh Bharat Abhiyan, which means "Clean India Campaign." It's like a big mission to keep our country clean and healthy.

One super important part of this mission is building toilets in villages. In some places, people didn't have proper toilets, and that's not good for health or cleanliness. So, they started building toilets in villages, like giving families a clean and safe place to go.

Another cool thing is they encouraged people to use fewer plastic bags. Plastic pollution is a big problem, and Modi wanted to change that. Using fewer plastic bags is like giving our environment a helping hand.

- Modi's Heartfelt Care for Our Health

Modi's initiatives are all about making sure we're healthy and our country is clean. Ayushman Bharat gives families access to medical care without worrying about costs. The Swachh Bharat Abhiyan is like a mission to keep our surroundings clean and green. These efforts are like a warm embrace from our government, ensuring our well-being and a cleaner, healthier India for all of us!

Modi's Actions During Health Crises: Navigating the COVID-19 Pandemic

- COVID-19 Hits: The Challenge Begins

When COVID-19 arrived in India, it was a tough situation. Like a true leader, Modi took quick action. He urged everyone to stay safe by wearing masks, washing hands, and keeping a safe distance. It's like a reminder from a caring friend to protect ourselves and others.

- Lockdown: Putting Safety First

To stop the virus from spreading, Modi announced a lockdown. It's like hitting the pause button on regular life for a while. This move was to keep everyone safe and slow down the virus. But it wasn't easy. People faced challenges, like job loss and not being able to see loved ones.

- Helping Hands: Economic Support

Modi understood the financial struggles people were facing during the lockdown. So, he introduced financial aid packages. It's like a safety net for those who needed it most. This aid helped families make ends meet during a tough time.

- Vaccine Drive: The Hopeful Turn

As vaccines became available, Modi launched one of the world's largest vaccination drives. It's like a big shield to protect us from the virus. The goal was to vaccinate as many people as possible to build immunity against COVID-19.

- Challenges and Criticisms: Not Everyone Agreed

Of course, not everyone agreed with every decision Modi made. Some people felt the lockdown was too strict, while others thought it should have been stricter. Like any tough decision, there were mixed opinions.

- Modi's Leadership During Crisis

In the end, Modi's leadership during the COVID-19 pandemic was like a steady hand guiding us through a storm. He acted swiftly, prioritized safety, and supported those in need. It wasn't without challenges and differing opinions, but it was a time when strong leadership was crucial, just like having a trusted friend during difficult times.

Cultural and Soft Power Diplomacy

- Cultural Diplomacy: Making Friends through Culture

Modi thinks that showing what makes India special can help make friends with other countries. It's like sharing your cool interests with people from different places. He does this through something called "cultural diplomacy."

- Yoga Day: A Global Party for Health and Peace

Modi had a great idea – to create a day for yoga that everyone in the world can join. It's like having a big global party where people do yoga together. This makes people healthier and celebrates a special thing that comes from India.

- Indian Festivals Around the World: Bringing India Closer

Have you ever celebrated Diwali or Holi? Modi wanted people from other countries to enjoy these festivals too. So, he told Indian embassies to organize special events. It's like sharing a taste of India's joy with people from all over.

- Connecting with Indians Abroad: Like Talking to Faraway Family

Many Indians live in other countries, and Modi thinks of them as part of a big Indian family. He keeps in touch with them, just like chatting with family who live far away. He appreciates the good things they do and keeps the connection strong.

- Preserving Our Heritage: Taking Care of Our History

Modi knows that it's important to keep India's history safe. He started projects to fix old buildings and temples that are part of our history. It's like fixing up your grandparent's house to keep their stories alive.

- Modi's Global Sharing

To sum it up, Modi's efforts to share India's culture and history with the world are like adding colorful threads to a big global tapestry. He does this through cultural diplomacy, celebrates Yoga Day, shares Indian festivals, stays close to Indians abroad, and takes care of our history. It's all about sharing India's wonderful things with people from all over the world, making friends, and spreading happiness.

- Modi's Global Influence: Sharing India's Culture and Yoga

Modi believes that sharing art and culture can help countries become friends. It's like when you visit a friend's house, and they introduce you to their family's traditions, music, and dances. These cultural exchanges help people from different countries understand and like India's rich culture.

- Yoga Diplomacy: Spreading Health and Inner Peace

One of Modi's big ideas is Yoga Diplomacy. He suggested having a special day for yoga at the United Nations, and many countries agreed. It's like having a worldwide yoga party! On this day, people all over the world do yoga together. It's not just about getting healthy; it's also about celebrating a special Indian practice.

- Impact on India's Soft Power: Becoming More Likable

Now, let's talk about soft power. It's like being so cool and friendly that everyone wants to hang out with you. India's soft power comes from its culture and values. Modi's initiatives have made India even more likable to the world.

By sharing our culture and yoga, Modi has made people from different countries feel closer to India. This can lead to better friendships, more trade, and working together on different things.

- Modi's Global Influence

In the end, Modi's efforts to share India's culture and yoga with the world have made a big impact. It's like inviting the world to explore India's unique traditions and practices. This has helped India become even more popular and friendly on the global stage, which can lead to better relationships and partnerships with other countries.

CHAPTER 9

Leadership Characteristics

Strong leadership skills are necessary to achieve great responsibilities. Whether you manage a business organization, a small office team, or politics, leadership development is crucial. These skills help increase productivity, create a culture of trust, and improve harmony. The development of this internal quality is the guarantee of success.

Despite its humble beginnings, Modi's unparalleled leadership helped rise to the level of success. From fulfilling social responsibilities to entering Indian politics, Modi has demonstrated great leadership skills. Leadership and management are closely related and both affect a person's work and personal life. Being a smart leader, Modi used these two traits to succeed in his job.

Modi is known for his thirst for leadership. From moving the Tata Nano car company to Gujarat, openly inviting Ratan Tata to the state, inviting Bollywood superstar Amitabh Bachchan as the chief minister of Gujarat, there is the politics of Narendra Modi, always showing an unprecedented culture. He inspired Ratan Tata, who was trying to open a factory in West Bengal, with an SMS invitation.

Unlike other politicians who use the beauty of Bollywood to promote their parties and campaigns, Narendra Modi asked Bachchan to talk about the sacred sands of Kutch Farm, Somnath temple, ancient times of Harappan civilization, attracting lions and encouraging tourists. The wonderful land of Gujarat. These examples strongly demonstrate that Modi's unique leadership style combines long-term planning and focus. Modi himself set the target and presented a program to achieve it at all levels. Modi's critics and supporters often view his leadership as focused on the power he wields. Being a leader is something Modi can do. A real leader should be honest, patient, generous, be able to lead by example and be the first to make a sacrifice. This is exactly what Modi is doing in all his initiatives.

Modi displayed his leadership qualities after registering record wins in the Vadodara and Varanasi elections. In baroda, sought help from the party.

In his heartfelt speech Modi said that the government does not belong to any political party but to all the people of this country. Management is the key to success in one's life. Generally speaking, people take pride in every small achievement they achieve in life. These small successes become "everything" in their lives. This is Modi's advantage over other politicians of the same ilk. Criticism is the greatest test for a leader. Modi is no different. He was forced to resign from his seat after the 2002 Gujarat riots.

But nothing can stop the leader. A teacher who overcomes criticism with a good topic – Modi A political expert is someone who knows everything. For example, the BJP he leads has won the Gujarat elections three times. Church members view him as the leader best suited to the important task of election and campaign management. The historic victory of Narendra Modi-led Bharatiya Janata Party in the 2012 Gujarat elections was appreciated at home and abroad! Modi has achieved great success in Gujarat as an impartial and effective leader. Many believe that Modi's skills and abilities are limited to ruling Gujarat. Although he demonstrated great political ability in Gujarat, there were doubts about his ability to rule the rest of the country.However, this is just an assumption and misinformation. There are many examples of leaders who overcame adversity and emerged victorious. big. Advani resigned from all his positions soon after Modi was announced as leader of the ruling Bharatiya Janata Party. Modi had to face opposition from members of his own party. Advani later withdrew his resignation. In another example, the Bihar-based Jana Dal (JDU) announced the end of its 17-year political alliance with the Bharatiya Janata Party (BJP). These two examples can destroy the spirit of a political leader. They also left a very deep impression on me. But true leaders cannot stand firm even in difficult times. He needs to stay focused. Modi has also demonstrated leadership awareness, maturity and wisdom by handling these adverse incidents and other challenges in his career with grace and calm. Modi has shown restraint in dealing with the opposition. This created a wave of confidence in the RSS, which affected the functioning of the BJP. As a result, Modi won the party's presidential election. These leaders are embarking on a new and challenging journey. Political candidate Modi (not yet Prime Minister) created an uproar across the country. There are still voices criticizing Victim and Rival Politics It is difficult to catch a leader in Elections are an example of the Janata Party. The results were great. The leader has turned into a superhero as he leads the majority party, the Bharatiya Janata Party (BJP). For the first time in three years, a political party has enough seats in parliament to form its own government. All the election efforts paid off and helped Modi become a target for political humanity. Prime Minister Modi has nearly broken world records for the number of rallies and protests since he announced his candidacy six months before the election. Opposition leaders like Rahul Gandhi, Sonia Gandhi, Mulayam Singh Yadav and Arvind Kejriwal have no place in the election race. Modi was appointed Prime Minister on September 13, 2013. Afterwards, he started traveling throughout India. During this tour, he faced many new challenges, 3D challenges and a special show called "Chai Pe Charcha". In total, the administration announced more than 5,827 new jobs. Narendra Modi addressed 437 public protests across 300,000 km of the country. This election is considered the biggest in Indian history. This included the Bharat Vijay rally, which began in Jammu and Kashmir, offered prayers at the Vaishno Devi Temple, and ended in Ballia (Uttar Pradesh). Modi also mentioned on his personal blog that the experience was very rewarding and interesting. Modi's unique attempt to connect with the public is his massive 'chai pe charcha' presentation. DTH is a unique combination of satellite, internet and mobile communications. It is broadcast in 4,000 regions nationwide. Modi is building relationships with these sectors by engaging in dialogue with citizens and listening to their concerns. Smart Indian managers know that they cannot compete in every industry alone, so they make full use of advanced technologies. Create a 3D video campaign. About 1,350 3Ds attended the rally. The protest was so popular that thousands of young people emailed their leaders on social media thanking them.

No one is too crazy. One of the most important aspects of Modi's leadership is that he never misses an opportunity to use technology to support national development and prosperity. For the first time in Indian election history, the Bharatiya Janata Party India has launched the a272 Mission App website. It provides an online platform where people can collaborate, contribute, donate and organize events. The platform also facilitates individual communication with competitors and competition participants. Living up to his reputation as a "modern leader," Modi uniquely harnessed the power of social media in his election campaign. He uses Twitter and other social networks to communicate. It benefits the people of the country and supports itself and its party. Prime Minister Modi took a selfie with his index finger after voting in Ahmedabad. The leader created a mosaic of Narendra Modi using a voter's selfie and an image of ink on his finger, which created waves on Twitter with the hashtag #SelfieWithModi. Prime Minister Modi also expressed support for the media during his election campaign. Interviews were conducted through a variety of print and electronic media. Although Modi has always disliked the media, he did not shy away from interacting with it during his election campaign. This shows what a great president he is. Harness the media the party needs and leverage the power of technology to a degree that cannot be achieved directly. Leadership is an important part of effective management. Political parties can achieve great success under the guidance of experts. Modi proved his enormous potential in this general election. His leadership and wisdom helped the BJP to keep winning. NDA won 335 seats in the 16th National Assembly. The BJP won the majority, winning 283 seats. The Modi forces returned the Bharatiya Janata Party to power after 10 years. After 1984, the BJP was the first political party to oppose his rule. In 1984, Rajiv Gandhi-led Congress won 400 seats. But the credit here does not belong to Gandhi's leadership. This was the only show of mercy since Indira Gandhi was assassinated that same year. Modi received a warm welcome in India's Hindi heartlands: Bihar, Uttar Pradesh, Rajasthan, Madhya Pradesh, Haryana, Chhattisgarh, Himachal Pradesh, Delhi, Jharkhand and Uttarakhand. This is evidenced by the historic victory of the BJP in these states, winning 190 out of 225 seats. Modi's magic department operated not only in his home state of Gujarat but also in central states such as Karnataka, Maharashtra and Assam. In the last National Assembly, the BJP had 116 lawmakers and 18.8% of the votes. On the other hand, the National Assembly has 206 members and a vote rate of 28.55%. Due to Modi's misgovernance, the BJP got 31.4% votes while the Congress got 19.5% votes. Modi's forces helped the Bharatiya Janata Party achieve three decades of victory and oust India's oldest ruling party, the Congress, from the Indian political system. The UPA won about 61 seats in the Congress administration. Unfortunately, the party failed to garner enough votes to help its leader become a Lok Sabha candidate. On the other hand, the Uttar

Pradesh NDA won 71 out of 80 seats in the 2014 elections, indicating that the state government fully supported the Modi faction, also known as the tsunami faction. Modi's magic is enough to defeat his enemies. Former President Mayawati's Samajwadi Party remains banned from opening accounts, while the Congress and Samajwadi Party have ruled that the state can contest only from family seats. While Sonia Gandhi won the Rae Bareli election by a margin of 3.52 million votes, Rahul Gandhi won the Amethi election by a margin of 4,444 votes, with a margin of 1 million votes. Samajwadi Party leader Mulayam Singh Yadav won from Mainpuri and Azamgarh. He later introduced his nephew Tej Pratap Singh Yadav. Long, long, long, long, long, long, long. Show your excellent management skills and leadership qualities by winning both Varanasi and Vadodara states simultaneously. Despite his legendary success. On the same day, Prime Minister Modi, who had promised simultaneous presidents of both states, visited Vadodara and expressed his gratitude to the voters. Not all of them. Prime Minister Modi dealt harshly with opposition leaders and defeated them in the elections by appealing to them for support and promising to work equally for all. There is much to learn from Modi's commitment to the country and its people. Efforts are constantly being made to take the concept of success to the next level. Modi's speech in Vadodara clearly demonstrated his incredible leadership abilities. After the victory, 570,000 people expressed their gratitude to the citizens.

Modi emphasized the importance of the victory and said it was the first time since independence that a non-Congress party had won a majority without its mandate. He continued his speech as follows: "In freedom, there is no enemy, there is a rival. This competition is the beauty of our freedom. The 'pain' ends with the choice." Modi is a true leader in every respect. His work ethic, common sense, long-term planning, and hard work to make his plans a success make him a great leader.

CHAPTER 10

"Modi's Political Journey: From Janata Party Chaos to Gujarat's KHAM Strategy"

Modi's life was about to change and expand. After the emergency, his situation became even more obvious. He had impressed his colleagues in the underground struggle with his dedication, and now he would be rewarded. One of the reasons for Modi's role in managing GLSS with outsiders is that Modi is introduced to those interested in national politics. They destroyed the goodwill of Pracharak, a young and working Gujarati. He was appointed as "sambhaag pracharak" (in the district association) in 1978. This was a big responsibility for a young person (he was twenty-eight), but he admitted that he was already considered a capable and reliable leader. Modi received RSS briefings in the vibhaags (administrative areas) of Surat and Vadodara "during his extended run from Kheda district in central and south Gujarat to Umergaon in Valsad". The job once again required almost constant travel, something he had become accustomed to and loved. Foreign connections disrupted his career in early 1979 when he was summoned to Delhi by senior RSS member Dattopant Thangadi, with whom he had already established a friendship in the field. Modi wanted to investigate and document the RSS ED. He has written a book on the subject of Gujarat but does not mention its use to prevent emergencies for many people, including people from other countries. Political parties and movements. This also means that he has been neglecting his work in Gujarat for some time, perhaps putting his recent gains in the state RSS at risk. But for his first entry into the country, the organization at the Delhi level has a balance in that regard despite being the controller behind the scene," as he always half-jokes in private conversations. Modi saw the opportunity for what it was and, accustomed to travelling light, jumped on a Delhi-bound train with only a suitcase and the promise of a room at a friend's place where he rested on layovers from his trips to all corners of India. Back in Delhi after a fact finding research journey, Modi collated interviews and documents preparatory to composing the text of the book. What he also had was a ringside seat from which to wince at the self-defeating quarrels and infighting that would tear the Janata Party alliance to pieces. This made a deep and abiding impression on him, and introduced a vital word to his political lexicon: discipline. Modi understood from what he saw of ideological quibbling, egotism and other unedifying displays of political selfishness that discipline was the only way to achieve anything. As Morarji Desai's administration squandered a historic opportunity to change the course of Indian history, Modi was privately formulating a practical ethic of political service he would apply to his own career. An important element of it was the stress on 'practical' at the expense of 'ideological'. As an aspiring administrator more than a politician, he gained an essential insight: that it was more important to understand a situation from all angles than to argue over narrow points of theory and miss half of the overall picture.

Vajpayee, as leader of the Jana Sangh since 1967, had worked hard to hold the Janata Party together, but the inevitable collapse, when it came, was devastating. The Janata won only a single Lok Sabha seat in Gujarat in the 1980 general election. India did not at this time have any parties speaking up for the free market. The Swatantra Party had fallen away in 1974. India seemed only to have socialist dogmas inherited by freedom fighters via Cambridge University and the London School of Economics (LSE), which was founded by Fabian socialists.

Nehru's subsequent leadership of India after Independence in effect had bequeathed an allencompassing socialist outlook that was by now the national ideology. Even today the Representation of the People Act requires all Indian political parties to pledge allegiance not only to the Constitution but also to socialism. The clause, added to the Constitution by Indira Gandhi during the Emergency, was amended and strengthened by Rajiv Gandhi in 1988 and passed without any objections from the Opposition. It means in effect that if you are an Indian, you are legally bound to be a socialist or to vote for one.

What India's putative 'right-of-centre' had instead of free-market oriented economic liberalism as in Republicans or America's Britain's Tories was a nationalistic, traditionalistic, movement Hindu under the parentage of the Sangh Parivar. It was not only socially conservative but also economically conservative in that it offered no practical or free-market alternatives to Nehruvian socialism.

Nobody in the Janata Party, for example, had thought of getting rid of the licence-permit-quota system; it was simply taken for granted that it was the way things were done. If anything, Desai's government had been even more damagingly faithful to the centralist command-and-control system than Indira Gandhi's. An alternative way of seeing reality would take another decade to develop, and would ironically be released into the body politic by the Congress.

The fragmentation of the Janata Party meant that the energy of the political opposition, having failed in office, required new channels in which to flow, and new vocabularies to articulate their ambitions for the country. So it is no coincidence that the 1980 general election 'marked the point from which religious identity began having a greater impact on Indian politics'.

The reason it did so was partly because of the 'pressure cooker' effect of the Congress occupying almost the entire politicoeconomic space. As a result, Opposition energies went off in different, more cultural directions to find their identity and gain voter traction. It seemed the only avenue available. But it was also in direct response to the strategic machinations of the Congress as it set about making itself immune to political challenge.

The Bharatiya Jana Sangh (BJS) since 1951 had functioned as the semiofficial political arm of the RSS. After the collapse of Morarji Desai's administration, and having tried and failed to hold the alliance in place, the BJS was in an etiolated condition. It was stuck in a dead end. It had given up on the Janata Party and decided to reinvent itself, partly at the behest of Vajpayee, who became the president of a new formation, the Bharatiya Janata Party (BJP) or Indian People's Party, created in 1980.

The BJS had been a nationalist party for those seeking a nation, and in a way it succeeded only too well in its aims, as M.J. Akbar described: 'It began as the party of refugees from Pakistan. The robust economic and social resettlement of the dispossessed, evident by the '70s, paradoxically, liberated them from the party which helped them. After the high-drama blip of the Emergency and Janata Party phase, the BJP reinvented itself as a champion of a psychological rather than an economic need."

But a psychological need is as real as any other, and this psychological need was precisely the territory the BJP would occupy that of a receding Hindu identity, cut adrift by the domination of the political centre stage by the Congress, with its frayed Gandhian ideals of the holiness of poverty; and hidden behind the back of that supposed humble piety, lay the iron fist. The BJP, it was clear early on in 1980, would need to fill the patriotic vacuum created by the nihilism of Independence postsocialism; one with a 'continental' sense, the sense of belonging to a people specifically of India'. The new BJP's relation to the RSS which significantly at this point opened its doors to non-Hindus would be the same as that of the BJS: it would be the political arm of the parent organization, although they would be two different entities, and one could fraternize among both until one formally joined the new party. It articulated five main aims: nationalism and national unity, democratic development, Gandhian socialism (there was it appears simply no imaginable alternative to socialism), principled politics and genuine secularism still of course a much-disputed term.

The BJP would prove a sturdy and significant presence in Indian politics, and within two decades it would be governing the country. Yet its birth in 1980 was very much an idea awaiting fulfilment.

India in 1980, as in 1970, was about to enter a decade of turmoil and upheaval, marked by riots, military action at the Golden Temple in Amritsar, Indira Gandhi's assassination, an anti-Sikh pogrom and then the optimism over young Rajiv Gandhi's premiership that itself turned to ashes in consequence of, among other things, the Bofors scandal. Dictatorship had been tried and found wanting by the Congress. Clearly, another way to secure its uninterrupted governance of the country was required, and this involved. marketing itself (with special offers) to various sections of the population that would reliably vote for it. Vote banks were about to be born, and the laboratory for testing them would be Gujarat where, in the summer of 1979, Narendra Modi had returned.

Madhav Singh Solanki became the new Congress chief minister on 7 June 1980, ending nearly four months of President's Rule. He arrived with a massive majority of 149 seats out of 182 and a plan that would set Gujarat aflame and lead to years of increasingly destructive riots that set caste against caste and Muslim against Hindu.11 It would, though, secure a decade of Congress rule in the state by consolidating the votes of various minorities in the party's favour, splitting the BJP's Hindu constituency by dividing it along caste and class. It was a masterwork of dark political calculation, and one from which Modi learned important lesson.

Solanki, along with other Congress leaders in Gujarat such as Sanat Mehta and Jinabhai Darji, had the brainwave that political success, not to mention the moral high ground, could be claimed by identifying the electorate in terms of their social status rather than as had been the case political loyalty. This could bring in votes if the Congress pursued strategy of identifying the very poorest and marginalized most groups (which comprised 56 per cent of the population in Gujarat) and offering them incentives. In other words, paying, in one form or another, the supporters of other parties to vote for the Congress instead.

The vessel of this electoral inducement would come to be known as 'KHAM', which took the initials of the target communities: Kshatriyas, a 'warrior' caste which felt its historical glories were insufficiently supported by its status in modern society; Harijans, the underclass Dalits who remained largely unorganized and thinly spread, and therefore ignored by political parties; Adivasis, exploited forest dwellers and tribal communities often abused and used as bonded labour; and of course Muslims, most visible, the visible, vociferous minority, to whom the most enticing promises would be made to bind them to the Congress.

In one of the many ironic-reversals of Indian politics, the Congress in Gujarat had stolen the clothes of the Janata Party, for it had been Prime Minister Morarji Desai who had first proposed formal rights for Other Backward Classes (OBCs) through the Mandal Commission which V.P. Singh put into action a decade later. The aim had been to improve the lives of those groups in society seen to be lagging behind economically and socially. The underprivileged OBCs were to be allotted a portion of public sector jobs and places educational institutions. The proposal recommended a riot-provoking 27 per cent reservation. The report was hastily put on the shelf in 1980 by Indira Gandhi and forgotten about until Prime Minister V.P. Singh resurrected the recommendations in 198990, with predictable results.

As far back as in 1972, in Congress-ruled Gujarat, the Baxi Backward Classes Commission had been set up 'to identify socially and educationally backward communities that would qualify for preferential treatment' reservations in other words.13 It reported to the Congress administration in 1976, adding eighty-six groups of OBCS to the list of scheduled tribes and castes that already enjoyed 31 per cent reservations in Gujarat's public sector and in universities.14 Its findings were adopted by the Janata Morcha government in 1978, after the end of the Emergency.

Another commission for improving the lot of sixtythree minorities and backward classes who had been excluded in the earlier Baxi report was formed on 20 April 1982 under retired high court judge C.V. Rane. It reported on 31 October 1983. Fourteen months later Solanki decided to implement its recommendation of an extra 18 per cent reservations, bringing the total quota to 49 per cent. This was enacted immediately prior to the March 1985 Gujarat assembly elections, cynically timed to boost the KHAM vote.

Solanki reversed the Rane Commission's stress on the definition of OBCs by income and insisted instead on caste, ignoring its cutoff limit of an income of Rs 10,000, probably to lure the relatively prosperous Kshatriyas. The result again was statewide rioting.15 This sort of madness had gone nowhere at the national level, of course, and Indira Gandhi had shelved the Mandal Commission report precisely because she recognized its absurdities and dangers. For example, the minorities and castes identified were not uniformly unrewarded, and many people within various groups were doing well economically.16 There also existed, quite naturally, vast regional variations in their fortunes. In Gujarat in 1985, however, Solanki saw that there was political and electoral profit to be had in implementing his own version of the Rane Commission dations.

In the ensuing riots,17 which began in February 1985 during the assembly election campaign, the anger of the mobs was underlined by the shock that reservations were cumulative, so that if quotas were not filled in one year, they 'rolled over' to the next, adding to the reservations all the way to a possible 100 per cent. 'The thought that they could be effectively barred from all seats of learning was enough for upper-caste people to go berserk, wrote one author.'18 The army was called in, and the prime minister and the Union home minister had to visit Ahmedabad to try and calm the situation Nevertheless, twenty-three houses were burnt to ashes in the Dabgarwad neighbourhood and 180 people died while 6,000 were made homeless.

But OBCs were becoming persuaded that the Congress was on their side, and the effect was social polarization. As there was a majority of lower-caste voters, this suited the Congress perfectly: "This strategy was a conscious topdown effort to realign the social basis of the party system in Gujarat,' says one leader today. It was evidence too of how communal tensions in Gujarat were sponsored and nursed, because 'caste conflict can get morphed into communal violence through calculated political strategy'.20 But it also slowly brought new people middle-class Patels, Brahmins and Baniyas who opposed the reservations, to support the BJP, and would prove the first small stimulus party.

During the fraught early 1980s, Modi travelled around Gujarat as an RSS sambhaag pracharak, nurturing the organization in his designated areas. Just as he had had a ringside seat for the death throes of Morarji Desai's Janata government, so also he witnessed first-hand the chaos engendered in his state by the Congress strategy of divide and exploit. The KHAM programme would later evolve into what became known, paradoxically, as secularism practiced by political parties both at the Centre and in the states. They had in common the pious fiction of helping minorities and the poor. This was supposedly in the interest of making society fairer, when in fact political favouritism. Iwas aimed at certain sections of the population for electoral gain. In the 1980s, it was OBCs and Adivasis who were offered political benefits in Gujarat; later, on a national scale, it would be overwhelmingly and controversially the Muslim. minority, starting with Rajiv Gandhi unilaterally overturning Supreme a Court ruling in a simple divorce case.

What Modi learnt from the riots over reservations and the proto- 'secularism' of Solanki's Congress administration was a respect for the Constitution and its definition of secularism. Narrowly defined, secularism was 'understood to mean neutrality of the State towards all religions [and] bereft of positive approach towards all religions. The essence of secularism is discrimination of people by the State on the basis of religious differences'. The practical implementation of secularism had to apply beyond faith, because everybody knew religion existed in social space, and its difficulties most often were reduced to conflict between castes or between communities Hindu and Sikh or Hindu and Muslim.

In its wider sense genuine secularism meant treating all citizens equally under the law. The same laws had to apply equally to everyone for this to work.

The riots instigated by reservations demonstrated the danger of resiling from that principle. Such abrogations of constitutional principle introduced inequality of treatment to different communities. That these communities could often be defined by religious belief was secondary. Under the country's constitutional definitions, one was first an Indian, and only after that a Hindu or a Sikh or a Muslim or anything else.

Modi had plenty of opportunity, criss-crossing Gujarat on his motorcycle, to observe the damage caused by such an abridgement. The underclasses were rightly resentful of the way in which social advantages were always claimed by the upper castes; the upper castes in turn were protective of their wealth and position, and sceptical that any good would come of special treatment for those below them. Yet if all were treated the same way, how could anything ever change and progress be made? It was all very well being equal under the law in terms of rights, but then what could end the severe inequality and social injustice of India?

Modi pondered this complex problem and began to formulate his conclusions and remedies for it from around this time. When he became chief minister of Gujarat in October 2001, Modi would immediately begin to put them into practice. That he could do so speedily, and on a very wide front, was because by then he could articulate a political philosophy he has since made his watchword: development. It was from his habitual wide reading and observations a sambhaag as pracharak that Modi started to understand how nothing would ever change while the 'Hindu rate of growth' of the economy persisted under Nehruvian-style state socialism.23 Since Independence such growth had averaged barely 3 per cent p.a., not enough to make a significant dent in poverty, given India's growing population.

Under the licence-quota-permit raj the outlook of Indian political parties would never change. Inequality and poverty would persist if there was not enough wealth to go around; all that could be done was to take someone's slice of the pie and give it to somebody else. Why not, thought Modi, bake a bigger pie? The solution obviously was to produce more wealth, which would benefit every citizen. But that would entail an alternative economic model: a free market economy and, on the part of the government, investment in social and economic infrastructure to grant the poor a chance to prosper as well.

That this sort of thinking put him at odds with the Congress was obvious. But it also placed him in opposition to his own colleagues in the RSS whose outlook was equally conventional. It was an organization, in Modi's view, that provided 'basically human resource management on a national scale. If you have it on a national scale you have human resource management quality.' Its potential to create change was therefore considerable, and Modi had many new ideas. But still his career would prove to be full of friction over the years as he attempted to persuade his colleagues in the RSS, and later in the BJP, to accept and adopt them. 'Not a single proposal, not a single initiative, was appreciated,' Modi says of his experience at this time. Always there was resistance, always there were questions. But if I am convinced, I will prove the results. Then results will make them convinced.' He speaks softly, as we sit one evening in his office. The voice rises in cadence as he recalls the days when he would argue and cajole his seniors in the RSS to think as economic reformers rather than as mere ideologues. It would be a precursor to his growing rift in Gujarat with the Vishwa Hindu Parishad (VHP) and its leader Pravin Togadia. Development, not deity, would become Modi's leitmotif. 'It is a very democratic system in the RSS,' says Modi. "They debate for hours together, it's an open debate. The perception is absolutely wrong that they are dictatorial. They are very open to discussion.'

But Modi's experience in Parliament is that of an outsider because of his thoughts and the way he sees and approaches the issue. "I always sit in the back seat, not the front seat," he said. 'I listened to what was happening, but I did not participate in the discussion, it was just my situation. Most of the time I see that they cannot understand me. This is my first impression. Then I tried to argue, but they didn't argue with me. Article Article Article Article Bullying Article Article Warming to the subject, he said, "I'll give you a small but good ple." Chapter 1986 Chapter Our state is very dry, very severe drought Chapter Even cattle fodder has run out RSS decided to do some activities especially for cows and poor people. The aim is to raise money worldwide, and the issue is discussed for hours in open democracy debates. Suddenly, it was time to make a final decision. I raised my hand. The person sitting on the couch got angry at me. "You were silent from the beginning of our conversation for four hours, now you raised your hand when we were done. There is no time anymore, what do you want to say?" Modi recalled this incident with pleasure: I said, "If you don't want to listen to me, I will follow RSS discipline." But I have an idea. They know me very well. They said, 'OK, what do you want to say?' So I started: 'Why do we do relief work like this? Why do we appeal to foreign nations? What is the need of it? We are a nation, we have human power. Our whole relief work must be on the basis of our human energy, our nation, our manpower. We can use different types of strategies to do this. I gave you the idea: We have many branches, many saviors. I said to myself, give me the math. If we can collect something called sukri, which is sweet and very useful, we can collect sukri from every family for a month. We can get help from the train for six types of transportation. We don't need to store water for the cows, but we can move the cows' tanks from dry areas to green areas. The state provides free transportation. Then they thought for a while and said, "Okay, let's have lunch now and then we will consider Modi's advice." When we returned, my proposal was accepted. Initially, we wanted to raise Rs 1 crore for relief work. As a result of these projects, we have provided services worth over Rs 30 million. that conventional thinking was endemic in India at this time, both in the RSS and the Congress: everybody's thoughts flowed along the same well worn channels or grooves. Second, that there was no feeling or confidence that India possessed the resources fulness or resourceto solve her difficulties alone or to succeed on her own. Third, that there was a new way forward that required an optimistic reassessment and reorganization of their own resources (they were thinking of 'collecting' for relief instead of, as Modi proposed, 'giving service' by sweating their assets). Fourth, that a fresh way of looking at problems was required to enable this, a sort of lateral thinking: it was, for example, possible to bring cows to the fodder rather than fodder to the cows, but it had not been thought of because the rail ways ostensibly had noth ing to do with drought. The anecdote also encapsulates neatly where Modi's reputation for egocentricity and arrogance comes from, even though it is a simple and honest story, technocratic rather than heroic and in a sense bereft of ego. It is believed that the approval of Modi's arrogance is not due to his arrogant behavior. Rather, it is because he is not expected to speak with confidence as a politician outside the RSS and within the country. Perhaps much of the internal struggle stems from Modi's denial of the influence of class and family. To his social "superiors" he is still a new working class who thinks above his station. Of course, it is an election threat to Congress. He recognized the threat early. This partly explains the unprecedented and unprecedented political opposition Modi has faced since his three consecutive elections in Gujarat.

CHAPTER 11

Economic Reforms, Defence, and Social Welfare under Modi

1. **Digital India:** Modi wanted to ensure that even schools in remote villages have access to the internet and computers. This way, students can learn online and use digital tools for studying.

2. **Skill India:** He started a program to help people learn practical skills for jobs. This means you can get trained in things that are needed in the real world, making it easier to find work.

3. **Swachh Bharat Abhiyan (Clean India Campaign):** Although not directly related to learning, this initiative focused on keeping schools and their surroundings clean. Clean schools create a more pleasant environment for students to study.

4. **Pradhan Mantri Kaushal Vikas Yojana (PMKVY):** This initiative aimed to teach people skills that make them proficient in their jobs. It also encouraged entrepreneurship.

5. **Pradhan Mantri Vidya Lakshmi Portal:** To assist students in paying for college, he created a website where you can easily apply for loans and scholarships.

6. **Atal Tinkering Labs:** Some schools received special rooms equipped with tools and dedicated teachers to help students create new things and solve problems. It's like a place for young inventors.

7. **National Education Policy (NEP) 2020:** This was a significant change in how schools and colleges

teach. It focused on ensuring that students learn more than just facts and aimed to modernize the education system.

8. **Eklavya Model Residential Schools:** These are special schools for tribal children in remote areas. They offer quality education to kids who might not have access to it otherwise.

9. **Swayam and Swayam Prabha:** You can go online to a website called Swayam to learn new things for free. Additionally, there are TV channels called Swayam Prabha that broadcast educational programs.

10. **Infrastructure Development:** Some schools received new classrooms, toilets, and clean water facilities to provide students with a comfortable and safe learning environment.

Remember, these are just simple explanations of these initiatives. They were all intended to improve education and learning opportunities for people in India.

Skill India Initiative: Empowering the Workforce for a Brighter Future

The "Skill India" initiative, launched by Prime Minister Narendra Modi in 2015, is a landmark program aimed at transforming India into a skilled workforce powerhouse. This initiative recognizes the importance of skills and vocational training in bridging the gap between education and employment. Its primary goal is to make the Indian workforce more job-ready and globally competitive.

Key Objectives:

1. **Enhancing Employability:** Skill India focuses on providing relevant and industry-specific skills to individuals, making them more employable. It

targets a wide range of sectors, from manufacturing and construction to information technology and healthcare.

2. **Promoting Entrepreneurship:** Beyond job placements, the initiative encourages entrepreneurship. It seeks to empower individuals to start their own businesses, thereby contributing to economic growth and job creation.

3. **Inclusivity:** Skill India emphasizes inclusivity, reaching out to marginalized sections of society, including women, rural populations, and differently-abled individuals. Special programs are designed to address their specific skill needs.

Key Components and Programs:

1. **Pradhan Mantri Kaushal Vikas Yojana (PMKVY):** PMKVY is one of the flagship programs under Skill India. It offers skill training to millions of youth across India. Participants can choose from a wide range of courses, and successful completion leads to industry-recognized certification.

2. **National Skill Development Corporation (NSDC):** NSDC plays a crucial role in implementing Skill India. It partners with various training providers and industry bodies to design and deliver skill development programs.

3. **Industrial Training Institutes (ITIs):** The government has revamped ITIs to align their training programs with industry needs. Modernization and up gradation of ITIs aim to provide high-quality technical education.

4. **Recognition of Prior Learning (RPL):** RPL assesses and certifies the existing skills and knowledge of individuals. This is especially

beneficial for experienced workers who may not have formal certifications.

5. **Skill Loan Scheme:** To make skill training financially accessible, Skill India introduced the Skill Loan Scheme, which enables individuals to take loans for skill development programs with favourable repayment terms.

Progress and Impact:

Since its inception, the Skill India initiative has made significant progress:

Millions of individuals have been trained and certified under PMKVY and other programs.

Various sectors have seen the emergence of a skilled workforce, leading to increased productivity and growth.

Entrepreneurship has been promoted through initiatives like the Stand-Up India program, which supports small businesses.

Challenges and Criticisms:

Despite its achievements, Skill India faces challenges:

Ensuring the relevance of training to evolving industry needs.

Bridging the urban-rural divide in access to skill development.

Ensuring the quality and standardization of training across various providers.

Prime Minister Narendra Modi's Skill India initiative is a critical step towards equipping India's workforce with the skills needed to thrive in a competitive global economy. By focusing on skill development, employability, and entrepreneurship, Skill India aims to create a more prosperous and self-reliant India. Its success will continue to be a key driver of India's economic growth and development.

Economic Reforms and Policies

Narendra Modi became India's Prime Minister in May 2014. During his time as leader, he made many important decisions about how the country's economy should work. These decisions were meant to help India grow economically, build better things, and become more connected with the world.

1. **Goods and Services Tax (GST):** One big change was something called the Goods and Services Tax, or GST. This is like a single tax that replaced a lot of other taxes. The idea was to make taxes simpler, stop people from cheating on their taxes, and make it easier for businesses to sell things all over India.

2. **Make in India:** Another thing he started was "Make in India." This was like an invitation to companies, both Indian and foreign, to come to India and make things here. The goal was to create jobs and make India a place where lots of things are produced.

3. **Digital India:** Modi also wanted to make India more digital. That means using computers and the internet to do more things like paying bills or getting government help. The "Digital India" plan aimed to teach more people how to use these tools and make life easier for everyone.

4. **Jan Dhan Yojana:** Modi launched a program called Jan Dhan Yojana, which was all about getting more people to use banks. This way, more folks could save money and access insurance and pension plans.

5. **Swachh Bharat Abhiyan:** He also started a big campaign called "Swachh Bharat Abhiyan," which means "Clean India." The goal was to make India cleaner

by building toilets and improving sanitation. Cleaner places can attract more tourists and make life healthier.

6. Atmanirbhar Bharat Abhiyan: During the COVID-19 pandemic, Modi introduced "Atmanirbhar Bharat Abhiyan" to help businesses and the economy during tough times. This included various measures to support companies and boost the economy.

7. Infrastructure Development: Modi believed in improving roads, railways, and cities. He wanted to modernize ports and make it easier for goods to move around the country.

8. Financial Inclusion and Direct Benefit Transfer (DBT): The government wanted to include more people in the financial system. They used a system called Aadhaar, which is like a special ID, to make sure that subsidies and benefits reached the right people directly. This made sure that help from the government reached those who needed it.

Challenges and Criticisms:

However, not everyone agreed with these plans. Some thought that GST was too complicated at first and caused problems. Some also questioned if "Make in India" really created as many jobs as hoped.

Conclusion:

During Narendra Modi's time as Prime Minister, he made many important choices about how India's economy should work. His decisions aimed to help India grow, make it easier for businesses to operate, and improve the lives of everyday people. But whether these decisions were successful and what effects they had are still things people are studying and discussing.

Impact on India development.

1. Introduction:

Narendra Modi's leadership marked a significant shift in India's economic policy and development strategies. He came to power with a vision of accelerating economic growth, promoting development, and improving the ease of doing business in India. To evaluate his impact, we can assess several key areas:

2. Economic Reforms:

a. Goods and Services Tax (GST): One of the most significant economic reforms under Modi was the introduction of the GST in 2017. It aimed to simplify India's complex tax system, promote a common market, and enhance tax collection efficiency.

b. Demonetization: In 2016, Modi implemented a controversial policy of demonetization, which involved the sudden withdrawal of high-denomination currency notes from circulation. While the move had mixed outcomes, it aimed to curb black money, promote digital payments, and formalize the economy.

c. Make in India: This initiative sought to promote domestic manufacturing and attract foreign investment. It aimed to position India as a global manufacturing hub and create jobs.

3. Infrastructure Development:

a. Smart Cities Mission: Modi launched the Smart Cities Mission to develop 100 smart cities across India. This initiative aimed to improve urban infrastructure, enhance quality of life, and boost economic activity in urban areas.

b. Digital India: The Digital India program aimed to modernize India's digital infrastructure, increase internet penetration, and promote e-governance. It played a pivotal role in the expansion of digital services and financial inclusion.

4. Financial Inclusion:

a. Jan Dhan Yojana: This scheme aimed to provide banking access to millions of unbanked Indians, fostering financial inclusion. It set a Guinness World Record for opening the most bank accounts in a week.

5. Foreign Policy and Trade:

a. Act East Policy: Modi's government sought to strengthen India's ties with Southeast Asian countries to boost trade and economic cooperation.

b. Trade Agreements: India signed various trade agreements and engaged in negotiations to improve its international trade relations, such as the Regional Comprehensive Economic Partnership (RCEP).

6. Challenges and Criticisms:

a. Unemployment: Critics argue that job creation did not keep pace with the growing workforce, leading to concerns about unemployment and underemployment.

b. Agricultural Reforms: The introduction of agricultural reforms faced significant opposition from farmers who were concerned about the potential negative impact on their livelihoods.

c. Economic Disparities: While economic growth was observed, there were concerns about rising economic disparities and inequality.

Defence And Security

1. **Make in India in Defense:** One of the flagship initiatives was "Make in India," which aimed at encouraging domestic defense manufacturing. This initiative sought to reduce India's dependence on foreign defense equipment by promoting the indigenous production of arms and equipment. This not only bolstered self-reliance but also created job opportunities in the defense sector.

2. **Defence Procurement Procedure (DPP):** The government revised the DPP to streamline defense procurement. The introduction of new categories and changes in the offset policy aimed at simplifying the acquisition process, enhancing transparency, and expediting the procurement of crucial defense assets.

3. **Tejas Fighter Jet:** The development and induction of the Tejas Light Combat Aircraft into the Indian Air Force was a significant achievement. This marked India's success in designing and manufacturing a state-of-the-art fighter jet, reducing reliance on foreign suppliers.

4. **Rafale Aircraft Deal:** The Modi government finalized a deal with France to acquire 36 Rafale fighter jets. These advanced aircraft bolstered the Indian Air Force's capabilities and technology. The deal aimed to enhance India's defense preparedness.

5. **Cyber security:** In the digital age, cybersecurity is paramount. The government initiated various measures to strengthen India's cybersecurity infrastructure, including the National Cyber Security Policy and the establishment of the National Cyber Coordination Centre (NCCC).

6. **Surgical Strikes:** The Modi government displayed a strong stance against cross-border terrorism. The surgical strikes conducted in 2016 in response to a terrorist attack in Uri were a notable demonstration of India's proactive approach to counter-terrorism.

7. **Integrated Border Checkposts (IBCPs):** To enhance border security and trade facilitation, the government initiated the construction of Integrated Border Checkposts along India's international borders. These checkposts aimed to improve the efficiency of customs and immigration procedures.

8. **Coastal Security:** Given India's vast coastline, coastal security was a priority. The National Committee for Strengthening Maritime and Coastal Security (NCSMCS) was established to address these concerns and coordinate efforts between various agencies.

9. **Defense Modernization:** Efforts were made to modernize the armed forces by procuring advanced equipment and technology.

Social Initiatives And Welfare

1. Pradhan Mantri Jan Dhan Yojana (PMJDY):

Launched in August 2014, PMJDY is a financial inclusion program aimed at providing banking services to all citizens, particularly those without access to formal banking.

It encouraged the opening of bank accounts, provided overdraft facilities, and promoted financial literacy among the unbanked population.

The program helped millions of Indians gain access to financial services, insurance, and credit facilities.

2. Swachh Bharat Abhiyan (Clean India Campaign):

Launched in October 2014, this campaign aimed to promote cleanliness, sanitation, and hygiene across India.

It involved building toilets, improving waste management, and creating awareness about the importance of cleanliness.

Swachh Bharat Abhiyan contributed to significant improvements in sanitation infrastructure and awareness of hygiene practices.

3. Pradhan Mantri Ujjwala Yojana (PMUY):

Initiated in May 2016, PMUY aimed to provide clean cooking gas (LPG) connections to women from low-income households.

It addressed health and environmental concerns related to traditional cooking methods, such as using firewood and coal.

PMUY benefited millions of households by improving women's health and reducing indoor air pollution.

4. Pradhan Mantri Awas Yojana (PMAY):

Launched in June 2015, PMAY sought to provide affordable housing to urban and rural populations.

The program aimed to ensure "Housing for All" by constructing houses for economically weaker sections and the homeless.

It helped reduce the housing gap and improve living conditions for many vulnerable families.

5. Ayushman Bharat – Pradhan Mantri Jan Arogya Yojana (PM-JAY):

Introduced in September 2018, PM-JAY is the world's largest government-funded health insurance scheme.

It provides health coverage to over 100 million families, offering financial protection against major illnesses and hospitalization expenses.

PM-JAY aimed to make quality healthcare accessible and affordable, particularly for the economically disadvantaged.

6. Digital India:

Launched to promote digital literacy and bridge the digital divide in India.

It aimed to bring government services online, making them more accessible to citizens.

Initiatives like Digital Locker, e-Governance, and BharatNet sought to improve digital infrastructure and connectivity across the country.

7. Skill India:

Focused on enhancing the skills of India's youth through vocational training and skill development programs.

It aimed to make the youth job-ready and empower them to contribute to the country's economic growth.

CHAPTER 12

"Modi's Leadership: A Tapestry of Humility, Inclusivity, and Economic Vision"

Humility is one of the best leadership qualities; It is the virtue of being humble and not losing sight of one's own abilities and self. Humble leaders appear respectful, moral, and tolerant of all people. Humility is sometimes misunderstood because many people mistakenly believe that humility equals weakness, makes leaders weak and can be easily deceived. Actually, this is not the case. Good leaders know the importance of patience and humility and instill these qualities appropriately. They understand that they are being watched by their followers and teams. Humility comes from accepting that they alone cannot achieve all the goals set before them. Such leaders can never be proud or complacent, whether in a group, family, organization or country. They attribute their success not only to their own abilities but also to their team. They accept their mistakes and value other people's opinions. These people create an open and comfortable environment. In his book Good to Great, expert and author Jim Collins noted that when evaluating the most successful companies, he found the leaders to be quite humble. They share the credit for success and are the first to take responsibility for mistakes. Even though Modi is sometimes very proud, he respects others. Despite his habit of making negative comments about other politicians, Modi is also known for his gratitude and patience towards others. Nilanjan Mukhopadhyay writes in his book Narendra Modi: The Man, The Times that he interviewed Modi. He felt that Modi's interest in him was personal, at a time when political leaders are mingling with journalists and the media is using its power to treat and praise them. He does not seem to be influenced by the journalist's organisations, ideas or writings; The person's choice of words, general body language and speech caught the person's attention. Leaders involve themselves in this process. A leader who cares about his subordinates, never appreciates or accepts them, and always displays a proud air will be difficult to follow, even if he encounters difficulties. Most importantly, a good leader needs humility to be a good leader in the long run. Narendra Modi may believe in this philosophy and may have instilled this trait in him from childhood. Modi is a man of humble beginnings: from a middle-class family, he started working for the RSS at a young age, where he cleaned floors and prepared breakfast, and as a young man helped his father and uncle serve tea. house. Although Modi is filled with lust for power and authority, he has a humble understanding of life and therefore cares about others. An important aspect of humility is what one does for others. Whether it's someone with less power or someone who helps you get back on your feet, you should be ready to appreciate them. Sometimes humility and simplicity can be confused with perseverance. A broad mind, especially a strong leader, must be developed to see problems from a broader perspective. Leaders who can appreciate team members and accept their ideas are better retained. This not only makes managers more aware of the real problems around them, but also increases their productivity.

Modi is also a person who respects his teachers, mentors and elders very much and keeps his promises to them. An example of this was in 2001 when his childhood friend, the school president, invited him to the school's best party. Not wanting to break his promise, Modi rushed to Vadnagar from the nationally important Wagah border. After he addressed the ceremony, his teachers came forward to lay flowers for him, but Modi refused, saying teachers deserved the real wreath. Even though he started his years with RSS, he respects people who are older and more knowledgeable than him. Natalal Jagda, general secretary of the Rashtriya Swayamsevak

Sangh, is close to Modi. It appears that Modi took care of the Foreign Minister, picking him up from the railway station and carrying his luggage. In another case dating back to 1990, two Indian Railway Transport Service parole officers, both women, were traveling by train from Delhi to Ahmedabad. Since their reserve tickets have not yet been converted, they are asked to share seats with two young BJP politicians for a while. They talked about politics and history during the nice conversation and sumptuous dinner given by the children. When the ticket inspector couldn't find a seat, the couple sat down and slept on the floor. One of the two women, Leena Sarma, first mentioned the incident in her article in The Hindu magazine, an Assamese newspaper published in 1995. Sarma listed the names of two men: Shankersinh Vaghela and his younger brother Narendra Modi. Humility is also close to reality. Modi seems to understand this and, whether intentional or not, has cultivated a public image as a grateful man who respects others with a generous heart. When Modi was elected Prime Minister of India in May 2014, he was modest in his inaugural address. Appealing to the people and the spirit of humility in the country, he said, "I want to say that you have chosen your leader, and I want to ask my friends that you gave 60 years to a leader and now you have given 60 months to a slave." It makes Modi a good leader. Trusting others and transferring responsibility to them is also a sign of humility. Giving responsibility and authority also encourages employees to contribute their ideas. Let them decide to boost their confidence, as Modi did. When he became president, he demanded that almost all leaders in the political party give important roles to community leaders and told senior leaders not to take all the checks. Arrogance is a struggle for many leaders and it is the same for Modi, but accept that he is not trying. An important characteristic that distinguishes Modi from other leaders is that he remains humble and never becomes a victim of the flow of power in his mind. It often happens that when a person has more influence, it is easy to become a victim of this and humility is gradually replaced by pride. This is reflected in Modi's move to become president when he realizes that the son of a worker in the office has passed his civil exam; This is a small but important move. He invited father and son to drink tea and spend quality time together. Generally, leaders of all stripes in India are so dedicated that they are at least worried about someone who has no influence over them or financial interest, but the Governor was aware that he was not a Tier 4 staff. but he also does his best to prioritize them and make time out of his busy schedule.

Another important incident that shows his humility is that whenever he became the Chief Minister of Gujarat, he visited his elders and sought prayers from them. In fact, on the eve of the Gujarat elections, when Modi returned to the presidency with a majority of refugees, his old mentor Keshu Bhai Patel offered to form a new party. Modi visited Keshu Bhai's house for the first time to seek his blessings. Many people who know Modi say he maintains a sense of humility and humility that is often found lacking in powerful people. He has a sharp memory and often goes the extra mile to recognize and appreciate the efforts of those around him. It is an obvious fact that Modi has always been humble. He maintains a modest lifestyle, still does good for the locals, and ensures that justice and basic things are given the highest priority. Modi often undermines the established and important to be modest even in his work. Many people familiar with his work said that as president and now president, he created a platform for direct collaboration with secretaries and other officials, often lower in the hierarchy, to understand the issues they would face or the problems encountered. . She is in regular contact with her resident colleagues to provide them with the guidance and support they need for their work. In India's system of governance, which heavily influences the chain of command and hierarchy, Modi enjoys an open-door policy: an attitude that emphasizes his humility as a commoner and his respect for the business he leads. Of all the important qualities of effective leadership, humility is one of the most difficult to develop. It requires the person to accept his own flaws and to gather and appreciate knowledge from others. Among India's most loved and admired politicians, Atal Behari Vajpayee is the epitome of humility. Born in Gwalior to a family of teachers, he began his career as a poet and journalist and later became one of the country's leading political figures. Years later, even during his shining years as a politician and Prime Minister, Vajpayee always displayed graciousness for his visiting relatives as well as everyone else around him. Al Gore, a prominent American politician and 45th Vice President, in a speech delivered in USA spoke about Vajpayee among an audience of diplomats: "In today's world, it is rare to find a leader who combines the qualities of idealism and pragmatism, confidence and humility. In you, Mr. Prime Minister, we find such a leader." Vajpayee's inherent quality of humility is acknow acknowledged throughout the world. In India, he has been a prominent leader, implemented hundreds of developmental projects and still always stayed away from arrogance. He is also a man of simplicity. Sometime in 2005, the Indian government gave him a BMW car after his humble ambassador's car broke down. Narendra Modi took inspiration from the former prime minister in part because of Vajpayee's humility in public life. In addition to their humble beginnings both in childhood and early life, the men focus on politics, which includes their goal of raising the best people. Modi promised to continue and support Vajpayee's development policies in many areas, including Bihar.Even given Modi's authority and sharp sarcasm, it is difficult to imagine him being as kind to his opponents as Vajpayee. But Modi is likely to incorporate and use this trait more than he already has, due to his understanding of people and the importance of public relations. The best and most effective leaders often have a broad approach as the basis of their authority. Participation means involving and engaging everyone in the development process, creating policies that will benefit not only the privileged but all other classes. It involves creating an environment where everyone has the opportunity to participate in creating success and where everyone is valued for their unique skills, experiences, and ideas. Leaders in organizations of all kinds create work that is inclusive, comfortable, and empowering. These leaders are open to ideas, accept differences at all levels, and understand the importance of development. At the grassroots level, management is also about inclusivity, including input from all operational levels when making decisions or implementing strategies. Employee engagement and integration of diversity into the integration process is part of inclusion. It's something that needs to be done and it's a very good business model. The meaning of this idea, which is to make people self-sufficient, is incredible and not understood. Leaders may not be willing to share responsibility or authority, but because this comes from accepting personal limitations, effective leaders ensure that participation occurs properly. This approach has a great impact on empowering people and making them feel like contributors to the entire development process. Modi has been an advocate of economic development and has made it a key element of his vision to develop India. Our country is a thriving, diverse society, and to achieve this, leaders must strive for full cooperation and equality among the people. Modi has taken the first step in the desired direction by setting an inclusive vision. Sameer Kochhar tries to identify inclusive development models in his book Modinomics. "Beyond this, capacity building, financial support and support through democratic participation are at the core of our development and economic inclusion, as are social inclusion, digital inclusion and financial inclusion," He wrote. Modi's vision of inclusive growth. Including these three dimensions. At its core, inclusive development involves giving a country's people a fair chance to contribute to economic growth and being allowed to enjoy the benefits it brings. As Southeast Asian countries have proven, to achieve economic growth, growth must be inclusive. This means giving citizens the skills and education they need to succeed. Before Modi came to power, people divided India's participation more by region, race, religion, religion, etc. They understood from different angles. Aware that these trends are leading to the division of India, Modi is presenting an overarching agenda that is in many ways truly national in its approach and style. For sixty years, the inclusion approach has done more harm than good; It excluded people rather than included them. Part of this can be attributed to the personal goals of the government and its leaders, and part to a lack of business connections. By ignoring economic ties, Indian democracy has led to division and conflict among certain groups while benefiting only a portion of the population. But Modi has taken steps to include all sections of society during his tenure as chief minister of Gujarat and now as president of India. Section reached out to children (Section are generally considered members of the administration), North easterners, and people from different regions and businesses. Section Business development. Article Bullying Article Bullying Article Bullying Article Bullying The desire for unity was evident even when elected; He showed his trust in them by personally reaching out and uniting veterans, farmers, businessmen, women and youth. If his words and sayings are carefully analyzed, he always shows himself as a team player and calls on all levels to support him, which is just part of his dream of growth and development. the entire framework of development. In his national economic vision, Modi emphasized the importance of improving education, providing healthcare facilities, building railways and good communication. It also supports focusing on developing the manufacturing and service sectors to solve the problem of import-export mismatch. His view that e-government is the best form of governance is another indication of his openness to technology and his confidence in the important role of governance, which can lead to growth. Modi is conscious of the need to reach out to all groups and work for the welfare of all. In his speech in the Lok Sabha in May 2014, Modi talked about the importance of empowering all sections of society. It seeks to integrate the idea of "development" into a broad movement and make the goal of development the agreement of all citizens of the country. Firstly, this situation is reflected in the transfer of political power and the increase of the power of the state. Modi also seeks to integrate the Indian economy into the development of the country and emphasizes on human resources development because he believes in the untapped and untapped potential of India's youth. India's shortage of resources in terms of skills and talents should be a cause for concern because without skilled people to utilize these resources, employment is spared. Modi's economic vision makes sense; India needs good infrastructure including roads, power, ports, railways and general infrastructure. People want easy access to amenities, technology and innovation. While this concept is not new in government, Modi has brought a clear purpose and time to it with a strong sense of purpose, determination and desire to succeed. When people are involved it is best to be clear: have a clear vision, develop an action plan and let people know what their responsibilities are and what they will do, how this can be created. People, groups and communities without a cause will criticize politicians and governments for not understanding their role. Modi also believes in ensuring true secularism, where every citizen looks after the interests of all Indians and not just one community. He reiterated the principle that for India's progress "justice must be achieved for all and peace must be maintained for none". Modi believes that the Indian people must return to the old definition of secularism, that the identity of every citizen is his or her nation. He advocated "Sab ka haath, sab ka vikas" (everyone should be a part of development) and said that it was his right to work for the needs of everyone. Modi is often criticized for his actions that harm Muslims. However, when one digs deeper into the field records, it becomes clear that Muslims in Gujarat benefited as much as Christians of other religions. A 2013 report by the National Sample Survey led by Amitabh Kundu examined the situation of Muslims after accepting the Sachar report in 2006 and found that the percentage of people below the poverty line in Gujarat increased by 4,444. poverty line. It dropped from 42% to 14.6% in urban areas and from 31% to 7% in rural areas. At the same time, per capita expenditure reached its highest level at, with an increase of 39 percent and 27 percent, respectively. Chapter Instead, they have a partnership that will ultimately benefit everyone. Taking the state of Gujarat and its economic development as an example, it can be seen that the Gujarat government is pursuing an inclusive development process rather than targeting all ethnic groups, faiths or communities. In fact, it is said that for the minority in Gujarat, as well as the majority of the society, the economic growth of the poor in the "Modi" era has outstripped the rich. Panchayats are supported and function as Community Service Centers (CSCs) for employment generation and entrepreneurship. Modi is seen as a leader who can take action and empower people to achieve economic, social and digital inclusion. In his speech to the nation on August 15, 2014, Modi talked about the "Digital India" campaign he launched to encourage Indians to use technology in every field. One of their main methods is to encourage women by taking them online which will easily help by doing this online and effectively. Government services will also be delivered electronically to citizens to enable Digital India to successfully transform the use of digital infrastructure. Google India, where nearly 1.1 billion people do not speak English, has partnered with the government to help advance digital India by launching nine open source fonts in Hindi and will make the same text available in other languages. The same goes for Indian languages. Through these measures, Modi aims to make India a strong social and economic power, where technology is the key to change. As Prime Minister, Modi also launched the Pradhan Mantri Jan Dhan Yojana (PMJDY) on 28 August 2014 to implement it. The program offers the option of opening a zero-interest bank account to enable low-income families to make their bank payments. Over Rs 150 million bank accounts were opened on the opening day and the Prime Minister said, "Let's celebrate Finance Day today." The financial system inherently includes the goal of benefiting everyone without discrimination and provides banking and services, including insurance and debit cards, to everyone. This will also help the poor escape from the clutches of ruthless moneylenders. Providing financial services to Indians is considered an important step in India's economic and business development as it has led to a positive development for investors, businesses and financial institutions. For example, Modi also plans to build villages; eventually, he wants all Congress members to build model villages in their constituencies by 2016. from local structures near their areas. Modi expressed great concern and firm commitment to this movement so that the masses can access affordable financial services such as banking, credit, insurance, credit investment, retirement and financial literacy. An important question worth considering is how Modi's coalition differs from previous governments, which are also purported to be inclusive, poor-inclusive, and support Mnerga for a welfare model that most people understand is one based on cheap food and subsidies. . Unlike previous administrations, Modi's model is the most important: to improve the economic structure of individuals and families through actions aimed at the hard work of individuals and the ease of organizations. Modi's model of participation is different from the model that has been advocated time and time again since our independence, it is not a "grandmother" model; instead, it aims to give everyone a chance so that everyone can benefit. This model has some advantages because it does not separate the beneficiaries according to a certain culture or relationship, but opens opportunities for everyone. Proximity production or unhindered energy or reducing bureaucracy will provide jobs and economic benefits for everyone because it is based on energy rather than self-regulation. Modi also showed his unity by keeping a close eye on the situation and finding smart people as friends. While many say his approach is "Big Brother oversight", Modi encourages his colleagues to do better and show their competitiveness internally. He called for "minimum government, maximum governance" and expressed a desire for greater unity as India gradually shifted from the focus of independence towards leadership over the last six decades. It has now been proven beyond doubt that government intervention does not lead to power and time being in the hands of a minority and to the exclusion of opportunities and the management of public goods. In a country like India, where hierarchies and centers of power are important and political leadership takes a lot of time to maintain, Modi has shown little concern for them when it comes to integration. He could have chosen to abandon his NDA allies after his impressive victory in the general elections, but he chose to keep the herd intact. Likewise, by communicating directly with officer-level officials in the Indian bureaucracy and sending them direct advice, it provided them with an open line of communication that does not currently exist. Although many people think this is by design, many secretaries welcome it because they are often faced with the problem of deciding big issues and so many people are regularly excluded from politics or removed from the policy process. from. Many think this is really important and includes many views. Although many question his policies as arbitrary and capricious, Modi's policies and visions (mostly economic) have been clearly visible and have benefited people of all races, religions and beliefs. This is important for business leaders because they realize that the participation of all stakeholders plays an important role not only in the growth of the organization but also in the development of all stakeholders and people. An important difference that Modi shows in his call for unity is that he does not shy away from taking responsibility and wants his colleagues to work for the masses. Every Indian who opposes the government knows that the biggest challenge facing Indian democracy is cooperation with the people. Although there is great control and management, ordinary people do not have access to state officials and leaders, they can only live in their own castles, around a small circle. Access to governance is limited to those in power or those who know those in power. Modi is aware that this is a limitation of his overarching agenda and has ensured that government officials and colleagues can communicate with the public by deferring work and keeping the government's purpose in mind. Modi himself has exemplified the benefit of using technology and other media to stay in touch with people. This is a unique display of unity and transparency, something that is lacking in Indian governance.

Chapter 13

Global Diplomacy and Impactful Policies

Digital India And Technology

Prime Minister Narendra Modi has played a significant role in shaping India's digital landscape and advancing technology during his tenure. His influence can be seen in various aspects:

1. **Digital India Campaign:** Narendra Modi launched the ambitious Digital India campaign in 2015, which aimed to transform India into a digitally empowered society and knowledge economy. This initiative has been instrumental in bridging the digital divide by promoting widespread internet connectivity and digital literacy across the country.

2. **Expansion of Internet Connectivity:** Under Modi's leadership, several initiatives were undertaken to expand internet access to rural and remote areas. The BharatNet project, for instance, aimed to provide high-speed broadband connectivity to over 250,000 gram panchayats (local self-governing bodies) across India, making the internet more accessible to the masses.

3. **Promotion of Digital Payments:** Modi's demonetization move in 2016 accelerated the adoption of digital payment methods. His government encouraged the use of digital wallets, UPI (Unified Payments Interface), and mobile banking, which led to a significant increase in digital transactions and reduced reliance on cash.

4. **Startup India:** The Startup India campaign, launched by Modi, aimed to foster innovation and entrepreneurship in the technology sector. It provided various incentives and support mechanisms for startups, making India one of the fastest-growing startup ecosystems in the world.

5. **Make in India:** The Make in India initiative was launched to promote domestic manufacturing, including electronics and technology hardware. This encouraged global tech companies to invest in India, leading to the production of smartphones and other electronic devices within the country.

6. **Promotion of Artificial Intelligence (AI) and Research:** Modi's government recognized the importance of emerging technologies like AI and blockchain. Initiatives like the National AI Mission were introduced to boost research and development in these fields, making India a hub for cutting-edge technology innovation.

7. **Digital Governance:** Under Modi, there was a significant push towards e-governance and the digitization of government services. Initiatives like the Digital Locker, e-Sign, and the MyGov platform aimed to streamline government operations and increase transparency.

8. **Cyber security Initiatives:** As technology adoption increased, so did the importance of cybersecurity. Modi's government took measures to strengthen India's cybersecurity infrastructure, including the launch of the National Cyber Coordination Centre (NCCC) and efforts to enhance cybersecurity awareness.

9. **Space Technology:** Modi's administration also encouraged advancements in space technology through the Indian Space Research Organisation (ISRO). Initiatives like the Mars Orbiter Mission and Chandrayaan-2 showcased India's capabilities in space exploration and technology.

10. **International Collaborations:** Modi's leadership facilitated collaborations with several countries in the field of technology. India partnered with nations like the United States, Israel, and Japan to foster technological innovation and knowledge exchange.

11. **In conclusion:** Prime Minister Narendra Modi's influence on Digital India and technology has been profound. His government has not only accelerated digital adoption but also fostered a culture of innovation, entrepreneurship, and technological progress in India, positioning the country as a global tech player.

Foreign Relations

Narendra Modi's foreign relations during his tenure as India's Prime Minister, covering bilateral and global diplomacy, as well as relations with neighboring countries.

Bilateral and Global Diplomacy during Modi's Tenure (50 points):

Bilateral Diplomacy:

1. United States: Modi's rapport with U.S. Presidents Barack Obama and Donald Trump led to strengthened ties in defense, counterterrorism, and trade.

2. Russia: Annual summits with Russian President Vladimir Putin have deepened defense, energy, and strategic partnerships.

3. China: Efforts to enhance economic ties with China were balanced against border disputes in regions like Doklam and Ladakh.

4. Israel: Modi's historic visit to Israel in 2017 resulted in agreements in defense, agriculture, and technology.

5. Japan: The "Special Strategic and Global Partnership" with Japan has led to infrastructure investments and high-speed rail projects.

6. France: Relations with France strengthened through defense deals, including the purchase of Rafale fighter jets.

7. United Kingdom: Modi worked on strengthening economic and trade ties with the UK.

8. Saudi Arabia: Relations with Saudi Arabia improved, focusing on energy security and investments.

9. UAE: Significant investments in infrastructure and renewable energy strengthened India's ties with the UAE.

10. South Korea: Bilateral relations with South Korea grew, particularly in technology partnerships, defense, and cultural exchanges.

11. Vietnam: Closer ties with Vietnam included defense and security cooperation, along with shared concerns about regional stability.

12. Australia: Modi worked on ties with Australia in areas like trade, education, and defense, and both nations are part of the Quad.

13. Brazil: Cooperation in agriculture and space research has deepened relations with Brazil.

14. South Africa: Agreements in trade, investment, and people-to-people exchanges have reinforced India's historical ties with South Africa.

15. Maldives: Efforts have been made to strengthen ties with the Maldives, focusing on maritime security and infrastructure development.

Global Diplomacy:

1. UNSC Non-Permanent Seat: India won a non-permanent seat on the United Nations Security Council (UNSC), enhancing its global diplomatic role.

2. SCO Membership: India became a full member of the Shanghai Cooperation Organization (SCO), increasing its involvement in regional security and economic cooperation.

3. India-Africa Forum Summit: India's relations with African countries deepened through trade, investment, and capacity-building efforts.

4. Indo-Pacific Strategy: Modi's government advocated for a free and open Indo-Pacific, aligning with like-minded nations.

5. Cyber security: India has cooperated with other nations to combat cyber threats and promote responsible cyber behavior.

6. Space Diplomacy: ISRO launched numerous satellites for various countries, enhancing space diplomacy.

7. Cultural Diplomacy: Initiatives like the International Day of Yoga showcased India's soft power.

8. Relations with Neighbouring Countries

9. Pakistan: Tensions with Pakistan persisted, with cross-border incidents and limited dialogue.

10. China: India's relations with China saw fluctuations, with border disputes in the Himalayan region leading to occasional tensions.

11. Nepal: Relations with Nepal faced challenges due to border disputes, especially regarding the Kalapani region.

12. Bangladesh: Modi's government strengthened ties with Bangladesh through land boundary agreements and cooperation in various sectors.

13. Sri Lanka: Efforts to enhance ties with Sri Lanka focused on economic cooperation, connectivity, and people-to-people exchanges.

14. Bhutan: Relations with Bhutan remained strong, marked by development projects and strategic cooperation.

15. Myanmar: Efforts have been made to deepen ties with Myanmar, including infrastructure development and connectivity projects.

16. Afghanistan: India supported Afghanistan's development through infrastructure projects, humanitarian assistance, and capacity-building efforts.

17. Iran: Despite international sanctions, India aimed to maintain good relations with Iran, particularly in the energy sector.

18. Russia: Russia remained an important regional partner, particularly in the defense and energy sectors.

19. Central Asian Republics: Relations with countries like Kazakhstan, Uzbekistan, and Turkmenistan have focused on energy, trade, and connectivity.

20. Indian Ocean Region: India sought to enhance cooperation with Indian Ocean nations on security and maritime issues.

21. Southeast Asia: Modi's "Act East Policy" aimed to strengthen ties with nations like Indonesia, Malaysia, and Singapore.

22. Middle East: Diplomatic outreach to Middle Eastern nations focused on energy security and economic partnerships.

23. United States: India's strategic partnership with the U.S. led to closer ties in defence, counterterrorism, and technology.

24. France: Defence and technology cooperation with France expanded, contributing to stronger relations.

25. Australia: Both nations worked together in the Quad, focusing on regional security and stability.

26. Japan: The "Special Strategic and Global Partnership" with Japan led to investments in infrastructure and technology.

27. Brazil: Agriculture and space research cooperation with Brazil contributed to closer ties.

28. South Africa: Agreements in trade, investment, and cultural exchanges strengthened relations.

29. United Arab Emirates: Significant investments in infrastructure and renewable energy deepened ties with the UAE.

30. Canada: Modi's outreach to Canada led to discussions on trade and technology partnerships.

31. South Korea: Technology and defense cooperation with South Korea expanded.

32. Indonesia: India's "Act East Policy" aimed at boosting ties with Indonesia.

33. New Zealand: Bilateral ties have focused on trade and educational cooperation.

34. European Union: Efforts were made to enhance economic and trade relations with the EU.

35. Latin America: India expanded its diplomatic outreach in Latin American nations.

36. Israel: Modi's visit to Israel strengthened ties in defence, agriculture, and technology.

Narendra Modi's foreign relations during his tenure as Prime Minister encompassed a wide spectrum of bilateral and global diplomacy. His efforts aimed to strengthen India's position on the world stage, forge strategic partnerships, and navigate complex relationships with neighbouring countries and global powers.

Narendra Modi's Controversies and Challenges: A Detailed Analysis

Narendra Modi's political journey has been marked by both fervent support and fervent criticism. Along the way, he has faced a multitude of controversies and challenges that have tested his leadership and resolve. In this extensive exploration, we'll examine some of the key controversies and challenges that have defined Modi's career and delve into the strategies he employed to address them.

Controversies: Navigating the Storms

1. 2002 Gujarat Riots : One of the most significant controversies that has shadowed Narendra Modi's career is his handling of the 2002 Gujarat riots. Critics have accused him of not doing enough to prevent the violence, while others allege that his government failed to provide adequate protection to the minority Muslim community during the riots.

Strategy for Addressing the Challenge

Modi's strategy in the aftermath of the riots involved a combination of economic development and maintaining a strong grip on power. He focused on positioning Gujarat as an economic powerhouse, emphasizing infrastructure development and attracting investments. This approach helped shift the narrative away from the riots and toward Gujarat's economic growth.

Allegations of Authoritarianism:

1. Narendra Modi has been labeled by some as an authoritarian leader, criticized for centralizing power within the Bharatiya Janata Party (BJP) and sidelining dissenting voices.

2. Strategy for Addressing the Challenge: Modi's response to these allegations has been to maintain a strong image of leadership while emphasizing his commitment to democracy. He has used his communication skills to connect directly with the public, presenting himself as a leader who is responsive to their needs.

3. Economic Challenges: Modi's tenure as Prime Minister has seen both economic successes and challenges. The controversial demonetization in 2016 and the implementation of the Goods and Services Tax (GST) faced criticism for their economic impact.

Strategy for Addressing the Challenge: Modi's government has employed a combination of pro-business policies and social welfare programs to address these economic challenges. Initiatives like "Make in India" and "Digital India" have aimed to boost economic growth and job creation.

Challenges: Tests of Leadership

1. Foreign Relations: Managing India's relationships with neighbouring countries, particularly Pakistan and China, has been a significant foreign policy challenge. Border disputes and cross-border terrorism have strained relations at times.

2. Strategy for Addressing the Challenge: Modi's approach has been a mix of diplomacy and a strong defence posture. He has engaged in both bilateral and multilateral dialogues while maintaining a robust defence infrastructure to protect India's interests.

3. Crisis Management: Modi has faced numerous crises during his tenure, including natural disasters, such as floods and cyclones, as well as the COVID-19 pandemic. Managing these crises effectively has been crucial.

4. Strategy for Addressing the Challenge: Modi's government has focused on disaster preparedness and swift response during crises. During the COVID-19 pandemic, he implemented a nationwide lockdown to contain the virus's spread and initiated the vaccination drive to combat it.

5. Political Opposition: Building consensus and managing a diverse democracy like India is no easy task. Modi has faced opposition from various political parties and interest groups.

6. Strategy for Addressing the Challenge: Modi has employed a combination of political manoeuvring, coalition-building, and a direct outreach to the public. He has used social media and mass rallies to communicate his government's policies and achievements directly to the people.

In the face of controversies and challenges, Narendra Modi has displayed a combination of political astuteness, resilience, and a clear vision for India's future. His strategies have often revolved around maintaining a strong public image, focusing on economic growth, and employing diplomacy when addressing foreign policy challenges. As we continue to delve into his career, we'll uncover how these controversies and challenges have shaped his leadership style and the trajectory of India's politics.

Narendra Modi's Prime Ministerial Campaign

Narendra Modi, the current Prime Minister of India, embarked on a remarkable campaign to secure the position of Prime Minister. Let's delve into the details of his campaign and his subsequent victory, leading to his appointment as the Prime Minister of India.

The campaign for Prime Ministership:

Modi's campaign for Prime Ministership began in 2013 when he was appointed as the Chairman of the Bharatiya Janata Party's (BJP) Campaign Committee for the 2014 general elections. With his charismatic personality and dynamic leadership, Modi quickly gained popularity among the masses. He tirelessly travelled across the country, addressing rallies and connecting with voters on various platforms.

Modi's campaign focused on key issues such as economic development, national security, and good governance. He presented a vision of a strong and prosperous India, promising to bring about positive change and uplift the lives of the people. His speeches resonated with the electorate, and his message of inclusive growth struck a chord with millions of Indians.

Victory and becoming Prime Minister:

The 2014 general elections proved to be a turning point in Indian politics. Riding on the wave of Modi's popularity, the BJP secured a historic victory, winning a majority of seats in the Lok Sabha. This victory marked the end of a decade-long rule by the Indian National Congress and paved the way for Modi to assume the role of Prime Minister.

On May 26, 2014, Narendra Modi was sworn in as the 14th Prime Minister of India. His inauguration ceremony was attended by dignitaries from around the world, signifying the global significance of his ascension to power. With his strong mandate and a clear vision for the country, Modi wasted no time in initiating a series of reforms and policies aimed at transforming India's socio-economic landscape.

Under Modi's leadership, India witnessed significant changes in various sectors. His initiatives such as the Swachh Bharat Abhiyan (Clean India Campaign), Make in India campaign, and the implementation of the Goods and Services Tax (GST) aimed to boost economic growth, promote entrepreneurship, and streamline taxation.

Furthermore, Modi's foreign policy approach focused on strengthening India's position on the global stage. He actively engaged with world leaders, forging strategic partnerships and promoting India's interests. His efforts resulted in increased foreign direct investment and enhanced cooperation in areas such as defence, trade, and technology.

Narendra Modi's Prime Ministerial campaign was marked by his dynamic leadership, effective communication, and a vision for a prosperous India. His victory in the 2014 general elections paved the way for his appointment as the Prime Minister of India. Since assuming office, Modi has implemented numerous reforms and initiatives, aiming to bring about positive change and transform India into a global powerhouse.

CHAPTER 14

The Journey To Prime Ministership To Re-elections

Narendra Modi's Time as India's Leader: The First Term

In the world of Indian politics, Narendra Modi's journey to becoming the Prime Minister was a huge moment. When he started his job as PM in 2014, it was a turning point for the country. In this detailed part of his life story, we'll look at the important things he did during his first time in office, like his big plans and changes in the country, and also how he started working with other countries.

Important Plans and Changes: Making India Better

1. **Make in India:** One of the most important things Modi did was launch "Make in India." This was a big plan to help businesses grow and create more jobs in India. It was all about making it easier for companies, even foreign ones, to do business in India.

2. **Clean India Mission:** Modi also started the "Clean India Mission." This was a big effort to keep our country clean and improve public bathrooms. It was a campaign to stop people from going to the bathroom outside and make sure our cities and towns were cleaner.

3. **Bank Accounts for Everyone:** The government started a program called "Jan Dhan Yojana" to make sure every family had a bank account. This was important because it gave people access to banking services and helped them save money.

4. **One Tax for All (GST):** Modi's government made a big change in our taxes. They brought in something

called the "Goods and Services Tax" or GST. This made it simpler for everyone to pay taxes, and it was the same tax rules all over the country.

5. **Digital India:** Modi wanted to use technology to help people in India. So, he started "Digital India" to make it easier for everyone to use the internet and digital services. This helped with things like getting government services online.

6. **Affordable Housing:** The government started a program called "Pradhan Mantri Awas Yojana" to make sure more people had a home to live in. This was about making houses that were affordable for everyone, whether they lived in cities or villages.

Working with Other Countries: India's Place in the World

1. **Neighbours First:** Modi's foreign policy was all about being good friends with our neighbouring countries. He wanted to work together, improve connections, and help each other. He also wanted to make India stronger in the Asia-Pacific region.

2. **Balancing Acts:** India had to be careful in its relationships with big countries like the United States, Russia, and China. Modi's government worked to make sure India's interests were protected while also being friends with these countries.

3. **Solar Power for the World:** India took a lead in solar energy by starting the "International Solar Alliance." This was about using solar energy to make our planet better and cleaner.

4. **Fighting Climate Change:** Modi's government cared about the environment. They went to big meetings about

climate change and promised to use more clean energy like solar power.

5. **Talking to Indians Abroad:** The government started "Pravasi Bharatiya Divas" to connect with Indians living abroad. This helped build a strong relationship with Indians in other countries and use their skills and ideas to make India better.

Narendra Modi's first time as Prime Minister was all about making India grow, improving the lives of its people, and building strong connections with other countries. His plans and changes aimed to make India a better place for everyone, and his foreign policies showed India as a responsible country on the world stage. As we go on with his story, we'll look at the challenges and successes that came with his leadership during this time.

Narendra Modi's Re-election in 2019:

The year 2019 was a monumental moment in Indian politics when Narendra Modi, a dynamic leader from the Bharatiya Janata Party (BJP), sought re-election as Prime Minister. This election wasn't just about one man; it was a reflection of the collective aspirations of a diverse and vibrant nation.

The 2019 Election Campaign:

Narendra Modi embarked on an extraordinary journey across India during the election campaign. His aim was to connect with people from various regions, backgrounds, and cultures. He spoke fervently about the progress and initiatives that his government had undertaken during his first term.

A standout program was "Swachh Bharat," or the "Clean India" campaign. Modi believed that cleanliness was not just about hygiene but also about dignity and pride. This campaign encouraged citizens to keep their surroundings clean, promoting a healthier environment.

Another significant initiative was "Make in India," which aimed to boost domestic manufacturing. Modi envisioned this as a path to create jobs, stimulate economic growth, and reduce reliance on imported goods.

National Security and "Main Bhi Chowkidar" (I am also a watchman):

In the realm of national security, the Pulwama attack and India's response in Balakot were pivotal moments. Modi's resolute leadership during this period reinforced his commitment to safeguarding the nation. The "Main Bhi Chowkidar" campaign symbolized that he considered himself a protector of India, echoing the sentiments of many citizens.

Empowering Rural India:

Modi placed a special focus on rural India during his campaign. He envisioned providing electricity to every village through the "Saubhagya Yojana." This ambitious endeavor aimed to bridge the urban-rural divide by ensuring that even the remotest villages had access to electricity.

Additionally, the "Pradhan Mantri Kisan Samman Nidhi" scheme was designed to provide financial support to farmers. This financial assistance was meant to alleviate the challenges faced by India's agrarian community.

Second Term as Prime Minister:

Narendra Modi's re-election in 2019 meant a second term as the Prime Minister of India. During this phase, he doubled down on his vision for the nation.

The "Atmanirbhar Bharat" (Self-Reliant India) initiative took center stage. This initiative aimed to promote domestic manufacturing, reduce reliance on imports, and make India self-sufficient. The goal was to make India an economic powerhouse in the truest sense.

Social issues remained a priority. The "Beti Bachao, Beti Padhao" campaign sought to empower girls by ensuring their education and safety. Simultaneously, the "Swachh Bharat Abhiyan" continued its mission to transform India into a cleaner and more hygienic nation.

On the global stage, Modi actively engaged in diplomacy, strengthening India's ties with countries worldwide. His participation in international forums like the G20 and BRICS showcased India's growing influence and relevance on the global platform.

Narendra Modi's re-election in 2019 and his second term as Prime Minister were marked by a visionary approach to development, unwavering commitment to national security, and a dedication to addressing pressing social issues. His leadership style and ability to connect with the people played a pivotal role in shaping India's destiny, both domestically and on the global stage, in the 21st century.

Demonetization (2016):

In November 2016, Prime Minister Narendra Modi announced a bold and unprecedented move – the demonetization of 500 and 1,000 rupee notes, which accounted for a significant portion of India's currency in circulation. The primary objectives were to curb black money, eliminate counterfeit currency, and fight corruption.

The impact of demonetization was multifaceted. On one hand, it encouraged the adoption of digital payment methods, reducing the use of cash and promoting financial inclusion. It also brought a substantial amount of previously undisclosed wealth into the formal banking system, contributing to a more transparent economy.

However, the sudden withdrawal of high-denomination notes led to immediate challenges. Citizens had to queue up for hours to exchange their old notes, affecting daily life and commerce. Small and informal businesses, which relied heavily on cash transactions, faced disruptions. The full economic impact and effectiveness of demonetization in achieving its intended goals continue to be subjects of debate.

Goods and Services Tax (GST) Implementation (2017):

The introduction of the Goods and Services Tax (GST) in July 2017 was a monumental economic reform. It aimed to replace the complex web of indirect taxes with a unified tax system. GST promised to simplify tax compliance, reduce tax evasion, and create a common national market.

The initial phase of GST implementation encountered challenges, as businesses and individuals adjusted to the new tax structure. The transition was marked by confusion and technical glitches. However, the long-term benefits became evident as the system matured. GST has improved tax collection efficiency, streamlined interstate trade, and contributed to economic growth.

Management of the COVID-19 Pandemic (Since 2020):

The COVID-19 pandemic presented an unprecedented global crisis, and Modi's leadership faced an extraordinary challenge.

In March 2020, Modi announced a nationwide lockdown to contain the virus's spread. This decision aimed to safeguard public health but had immediate socio-economic consequences. Daily wage laborers and migrant workers were disproportionately affected, with many facing job loss and financial hardships. The government responded with relief measures, including food distribution and financial assistance, to alleviate their suffering.

India also embarked on one of the world's largest vaccination drives to combat the pandemic. This massive undertaking involved distributing vaccines to millions of citizens across the country.

Throughout the pandemic, Modi consistently emphasized preventive measures such as social distancing, mask-wearing, and vaccination. The government worked diligently to balance public health safety with the need to sustain the economy.

In short, Narendra Modi's handling of major events, including demonetization, GST implementation, and the management of the COVID-19 pandemic, reflects a leader who has grappled with complex challenges. These events have had profound and lasting impacts on India's economy, tax structure, and public health response, showcasing his commitment to addressing critical issues for the nation.

CHAPTER 15

Financial Managementand Transformative Initiatives: A Look at Modi Government's Policies.

Financial management is an important part of management skills. This wisdom is very important not only in the world of politics but also in everyone's life. Financial management in a family, business or government is the key to long-term success. This is another area in which our President has mastered. No wonder Gujarat became an economically strong state under his leadership. According to the Prime Minister of India, the special development plans and projects prepared by the Modi government are exemplary. These powerful plans demonstrate the country's potential for progress and prosperity in the future. It is necessary to discuss the first budget of the Modi government here. This will help us understand our country's success in financing. The first budget of the Modi government for the financial year 2014-15 was prepared by Finance Minister Arun Jaitely. Here are the important details of the budget: Income tax exemption increased from Rs 50,000 i.e. Rs 2.5 lakh for citizens and Rs 3 lakh for senior citizens. Exemption for investment in financial instruments below 80C has been increased from Rs 1 lakh to Rs 1.5 lakh. Interest deduction limit for home loan holders has been increased from Rs 1.5 lakh to Rs 2 lakh. Commission to review all new tax provisions on indirect transfer of assets after tax reform, 2012 Budget deficit 4.1% of GDP for the current financial year and 3.6% of GDP for 2016 4 billion remains at the level. Used to improve women's safety in 4,444 major cities.

- LCD, LED TVs are becoming cheaper Cigarettes, pan masala, tobacco, aerated drinks are becoming more expensive.

- 5 IIMS HP will be opened in Punjab, Bihar, Odisha and Rajasthan IITS will be opened in Jammu, Chhattisgarh, Goa, Andhra Pradesh and Kerala. 4 more institutions like AIIMS to be established in Union, West Bengal, Vidarbha in Maharashtra and Purvanchal in Uttar Pradesh Government launches "Digital India" initiative to provide Broadband connectivity at village level National Rural Internet and Technology Mission to villages and assisting schools in preparing IT training Rs 100 New power and existing scheme supporting around 600 community radios Rs 100 for metro rail projects in Lucknow and Ahmedabad Govt expects Rs 9.77 lakh crore revenue crore from taxes Govt's plan expenditure pegged at Rs 5.75 lakh crore and non-plan at Rs 12.19 lakh crore.
- Rs 2,037 crore set aside for Integrated Ganga Conservation Mission called 'Namami Gange'.
- Kisan Vikas Patra to be reintroduced, National Savings Certificate with insurance cover to be launched.
- FDI limit to be hiked at 49 pc in defence, insurance.
- Disinvestment target fixed at Rs 58,425 crore.
- Gross borrowings pegged at Rs 6 lakh crore.
- Contours of GST to be finalised this fiscal Govt to look into DTC proposal.
- 'Pandit Madan Mohan Malviya New Teachers Training Programme' launched with initial sum of Rs 500 crore.
- Govt provides Rs 500 crore for rehabilitation of displaced Kashmiri migrants Set aside Rs 11,200

crore for PSU banks capitalization Govt in favour of consolidation banks of PSU.

- Govt considering giving greater autonomy to PSU banks while making countable them.
- Rs 7,060 crore for setting up 100 Smart Cities.
- A project on the river.
- Ganga called Jal Marg Vikas for inland waterways between Allahabad and Haldia: Rs 4,200 crore set aside for the purpose.
- Govt proposes Ultra Modern Super Critical Coal Based Thermalnology Power Tech.
- Expenditure management commission to be setup; will look into food and fertilizers subsides.
- Impasse in coal sector will be resolved; coal will be provided to power plants already commissioned or to be commissioned by March.
- Long term capial gain tax for mutual funds doubled to lock-in 20 period creased to 3 years pc; in-Rs 4,000 cr set aside to increase flow of cheaper credit for affordable housing to the urban poor/ EWS/LIG segment.
- EPFO to launch the 'Uniform Account Number' service to facilitate portability of Provident counts Fund.
- Mandatory wage ceiling of subscription to EPS (Employee Pension Scheme) raised. From Rs 6,500 to Rs 15,000.
- Minimum pension increased to Rs 1,000 per month

War memorial to be set up along with a war museum; Rs 100 crore set aside for this.

- Income from foreign portfolio investors to be treated as capital gains Investment allowance to manufacturing companies, to incentives small entrepreneurs.
- Rs I00 crores for development of organic farming.
- Indian Custom Single Window Project to be taken up for facilitating trade.
- Clean Energy cess increased from Rs. 50/ tonne to Rs 100/ tonne.
- Excise footwear duty on reduced from 12 pc to 6 pc.
- Net effect of direct tax proposals is revenue loss of Rs 22,200 crores.
- Tax proposals on indirect tax front would yield Rs. 7,525 crores.
- Free baggage lowance alincreased from Rs 35,000 to Rs 45,000/-
- PSUS to invest to over Rs 2.47 lakh crore this fiscal.
- The first budget plan under Modi Government is a classic example of finance management Most of the expertise.
- Constructed under this budget are directly associated with social welfare.

Now let us talk about the 'Jan Dhan Yojna'. Prime Minister Narendra Modi discussed about this plan while addressing citizens of India at the Red Fort on the Independence Day, 2014. This is an ambitious plan by Modi associated directly with the welfare of people of India. It has been launched with an aim to provide bank accounts to each citizen of India and help them gain the facilities offered by banks. The formal announcement for this scheme was made on 14ThAugust 2014 followed by an official launch ceremony by the Prime Minister of India 28th on 28 August 2014. Narendra Modi kickstarted the implementation of this scheme via sending emails to all the banks of India mentioning that the task should be considered as of Prime National Importance by their officials. He also asked them to be prepared for the gruelling task of opening around 7 crore accounts On the day of launch of this scheme, around whopping 1.5 crore a accounts were opened across the country.

The first phase of the mission, starting this month, would end in August 2015. Those who open accounts by January 26, 2015 over and above the Rs I lakh accident cover, they will be given life insurance cover of Rs 30,000. Each household get an RuPay debit card for POS sales and Kisan card. Upon satisfactory operation of the account for six months, the account holder will get a Rs 5000 overdraft facility.

In the second phase, all households that open such bank accounts under the Jan Dhan Yojana will get Rs 1 lakh accident insurance for 1.5 crore people. The poor face considerable out-of-pocket expenses in medical emergencies; in the lack of formal credit facility through banking channels, this pushes them into debt-traps.

In the year 2014, on the auspicious day of Navratri, Modi made a fresh start for India's finance sector Prime Minister Narendra Modi launched his flagship 'Make in India' campaign amidst much fanfare. It was announced on the Independence Day of India. The aim of this plan is to put India prominently on the global manufacturing map and, consecutively, smooth the progress of the inflow of new technology and capital, while creating millions of jobs. With this launch, it is clear that Modi is aiming towards eliminating the problem of unemployment in the country. He is also looking forward to attract foreign investments and ready to fulfil the requirements and demands from the business world to facilitate a positive manufacturing environment across the country.

While addressing the country on the launch of 'Make in India', Modi said, "In last 2-3 years, people talked of shifting industry outside the country. The focus of his government is mainly on physical infrastructure creation on top of creating a digital network for developing India as a hub for global manufacturing of goods ranging from cars to software, satellites to submarines and paper to power."

Modi assured his countrymen that the Government is committed to development. He also emphasised on the fact that this isn't a political agenda, but an article of faith and a mission for the welfare of the country. Here, Modi focussed on public-private partnership as well as skill development for boosting share of manufacturing in GDP.

In an assuring and optimistic tone, Modi said that the world is ready to set their foot on Asian ground and India offers best destination in terms of business because as it is a vibrant democracy with demographic dividend and enormous demand.

The Prime Minister said for him the term FDI for the domestic industry did not expand to "foreign direct investment" but "first develop India". So he told the citizens that the aim here is to create numerous opportunities of employment.

Elaborating the significance of 'Make in India' scheme, Modi ensured that his government has identified 25 key sectors in which the country has the potential of becoming a world leader. The Prime Minister said that he will be releasing separate brochures for these sectors along with a general brochure. The brochures will cover the major sectors such as automobiles, chemicals, IT, pharmaceuticals, textiles, ports, aviation, leather, tourism and hospitality, wellness, railways among others will provide details of growth drivers, investment opportunities, sector specific FDI and other policies and related agencies. Additionally, the government is also focussing on developing home grown industries and providing them an international status.

The ratings agency Standard & Poor's immediately upgraded its outlook on India's credit market from negative to stable, two years after a downgrade. The move is firing optimism for a revitalization of Asia's third largest economy. India's economy grew at an annualized 5.7 per cent in the first quarter of 2014, after staying under 5 percent growth for nearly two years, weighed down by high inflation.

The manufacture sector of India on which Modi is setting his dreams on is currently in shambles. According to statistics of World Bank, India contributed only 13% to the total GDP which lower than other smaller countries across the world including Pakistan and Bangladesh.

India is lacking in skilled manpower. The literacy rate is poor too. To tackle this problem, Modi stressed on labour reforms and skill development schemes for the success of the 'Make in India' campaign. He also launched six new labour schemes. It is said that China also started, 'Made in China' campaign. Modi may not have produced tax relief by introducing 'Make in India' campaign like China which exempted and gave relief on many tax related laws by introducing Made in China scheme. China and Hong Kong are leaders in the field of world manufacturing. India needs more efficient laws and schemes to be able to establish itself as a leader in the world of global manufacturing.

Modi believes that the promotion of villages is important for the development of the economy of any country. He also said that Make India Mission will be realized if the government focuses on literacy and provides other basic amenities to the villages. Keeping this in mind, Prime Minister Narendra Modi launched the 'Saansad' scheme on the occasion of socialist stalwart Jay Prakash Narayan's birthday Adarsh Gram Yojana" scheme to improve the lives of all classes. Improve the lives of people by improving basic facilities. Modi announced the plan in his Independence Day speech on August 15. It was later established by the Ministry of Rural Development. "Saansad Adarsh Gram Yojana" aims to help poor families escape poverty by developing strategies for all poor families. Gram Panchayat. He also assigned one of our members the task of identifying a village that was not his wife's village and making it a "model village" as of 2016, and two more villages as of 2019. "Model Village". After 2019, MPs must establish five model villages (per year) by 2024. According to the law, MPs must designate villages in rural areas instead of urban constituencies. The Yojna aims to transform villages into village structures through infrastructure, gender equality, women's dignity, justice, social services, sanitation, security, peace and harmony. Modi said that in this development plan, cooperation, self-confidence, local democracy, transparency and accountability in public life will also be ensured. Yojna will focus on promoting social relations and creating a good environment in model villages based on individual leadership and leadership of MPs. The District Registrar will manage the planning process of the Gram Panchayat, which will be a cooperative system. The plan focuses only on villages established for communities where families make up more than half the population. He asked the MPs to identify a village with 3,000-5,000 people living in the countryside and 1,000-3,000 people in the mountains to participate in the current economic development plan in the region. An independent time tracking network will be established for services covering all types and products in the country. The system will have an interface that allows MPs and other stakeholders to log in, give feedback/suggestions and even raise questions or complaints, to which the governing body must respond in a timely manner. All processes following the strategy will be photographed, geotagged and made publicly available. Likewise, images of all assets at different levels are also uploaded. The results of each project will be evaluated every three months against the material and financial targets specified in the local development plan.

CHAPTER 16

"Modi's Creative Leadership: Inspiring Trust, Innovation, and Mass Connection"

There are some universal qualities that successful leaders share; These include having a vision that will move their company forward, the desire to implement strategies, and the ability to increase trust. Trust is probably the most important thing a leader needs to achieve the desired outcome. Trustworthy leaders achieve better results because people follow their belief in their goals and thus do their jobs with more productivity, confidence, innovation and ethics. When people trust their leaders, they continue to work determinedly, believing that they can complete the task at hand. They trust leaders to make appropriate decisions, minimize risk, and take responsibility. As a leader, it takes time to build and develop confidence in one's abilities. Article Responsibility of the job makes one want to be careful Choosing a qualified person as a leader . Leaders should be genuinely concerned about the health of the organization Diligence and integrity Commitment to deliver and be able to achieve goals Believing in the ability of the leader Being able to trust them means they will work harder and more dangerously Because they know they have the support and trust of a leader Building trust Principles of Leaders must present knowledge clearly compassion, character, trust and wisdom. Their confidence in Narendra Modi by choosing him as India's 15th Prime Minister stems from their belief in him and his abilities. He presented his past contributions and successful ideas, gave ample examples to prove his efforts, and showed that he was willing to believe that he was the only leader who could help India achieve its development goals. We are inspired not by the ability to understand people, but rather by clarity, wisdom, responsibility and passion. People are reluctant to recognize someone as a leader unless they also trust their morality and integrity. Modi has been criticized for this, but he remains strong and confident that his plan can lift India out of current poverty. He also gained the trust of other world leaders. For example, recent talks with China and Japan led to the creation of plans under which both countries agreed to invest billions of dollars in India infrastructure development, energy production, railways because Modi was able to convince them of his leadership. by taking. initiate sex, ideas, satisfaction, hope and trust.

Trust as a concept largely depends on what matters most: being a leader who is confident in your ability to act and lead. Confidence is the starting point for spreading that confidence to others, not instilling confidence in others. Modi has demonstrated confidence in his ability to act and govern on his own, thereby setting a standard of excellence for others to follow. His confidence in his own abilities will show his faith in others, and those around him will follow suit. Chapter In addition to inspiring faith, true leaders trust their friends and followers, believe in their abilities, and give them the honor they deserve. Department heads delegate tasks and responsibilities to others. Recognize the need to delegate section tasks. Section "Employment". "Harassment" section. This is a clear sign of his great leadership. Take Modi's right-hand man Amit Shah as an example. He was one of the key strategists of the BJP political campaign in the 2014 general elections. In his address at the youth conference, Modi spoke about the role of youth in strengthening India. He trusts the abilities of young people. His commitment to improving education by providing vocational and other related courses to improve employability and career skills is just one example of his belief in the country's youth and potential. He also immediately and consistently demonstrated his belief in his party and his team, and in turn gained confidence in his leadership. Modi talked about Gandhi's principles of trust and confidence and said that the government should be responsible to the people and in turn should trust the people.

Addressing a business conference in New Delhi, Modi said the challenge facing India is not just the fiscal deficit but also lack of economic governance, lack of justice, trust, jobs and security and other deficiencies. Stating that this is everyone's responsibility, he said, "If we can create an environment of trust, India can get ahead of other countries." As Prime Minister, Modi encouraged the Defense Research and Development Organization (DRDO) to increase the number of young talents to 35. Scientists under the age of 15 ordered five laboratories. Modi sought to express confidence in the Defense Research and Development Organization (DRDO) as DRDO is known for its cutting-edge works. We believe that both they and India have talent. However, we need to attract young talent by providing researchers with the research tools they need. He also asked them to interact with ordinary people who are directly affected by their creations and innovations to get better ideas.

Likewise, he is considering sending DRDO scientists to universities so they can directly interact with young people, inspire them and develop new ideas. He called it a 'risk' and said he was willing to take it to give young people the opportunity to take on big projects and make important decisions. These beliefs about human resources often shape work motivation. However, this is not an ideal situation. With DRDO often described as "slow", Modi warned that competition from private sector companies must be treated fairly. To ensure this, Modi has also appointed the Minister of Defense to conduct a detailed review of the organization. Managers must motivate employees but also ensure that their efforts do not go in vain. In September 2014, Modi welcomed the international civil movement while attending the United Nations General Assembly in New York, USA. In an effort to connect with Indian Americans, Modi gave an inspiring speech to the crowd and truly showed his faith and trust in the youth. He said: "Some believe that the world is changing with the wisdom of the elderly. I believe that the ideas, new ideas, energy and 'can do' attitude of boys and girls are stronger." Modi's response to the "Make in India" call shows his belief in the Indian economy, its many problems due to China's aggression and its open trade protection. This shows his belief in Indian thought and capabilities. India's economic growth has slowed down since the last decade, partly due to globalization and mainly due to the impact of current policy on the Indian economy. Many studies have shown that Indian businessmen do not believe in investing in India and as a result, business and commercial confidence among businesses in society was at its lowest in the days before Modi came to power. Realizing that this is a major impediment to the overall development of India, Narendra Modi has initiated various reforms at the policy level, mostly in the controversial field of economic reform efforts, with the aim of not only making the body more productive but also more efficient. Promoting business management. system And say it.Modi made a public statement about production as he was aware of the important role of production in a populous country like India. Although changes in the work have been met with skepticism by many stakeholders so far, Narendra Modi has managed to manage the situation and asked companies not to see the work as a challenge. Competitors or people are off the table but work together to achieve the process of business success.

Therefore, Modi's aim is to build trust among stakeholders so that they can work together to achieve the goal. Section He reiterated his commitment: to remove the bottles and to be a supporter of this trust Section Harassment Section Harassment Section Harassment Section 4 Section 4 Harassment Working class can improve their skills to get a better chance in Section So that we can now grow the Indian economy to create a great difference and conflict affecting Section Chapter He Was Bullied Chapter He Was Bullied Chapter he was bullied His method was Alexander's defeat of the Persian King III. Similar to the method he used to attack Darius. Darius had an army of over a million men, and Alexander had an army of over a thousand men. However, he knew that Darius' army was slow due to its lack of fast horses and modern weapons such as bows and arrows. Alexander faced the challenge of a large army, using military techniques such as simple transport to defeat one of the largest armies known in the Western world at the time. Faith is not something created or inspired overnight. In his youth, Modi worked for several years in various positions in the RSS before gaining attention and the confidence to take on a more important role. This includes demonstrating competency by delivering results with consistency and loyalty. After years of hard work and seeing results, he could believe that he was a worthy candidate to become the Prime Minister of this country. The people of one of the world's largest democracies believe and trust him. Leaders must understand the importance of trust, lead by example, and convince followers that they are the true path. Without this trust, a leader's time will be limited. People in power often draw a line between good and bad intentions. History is full of examples of people who did not believe in most political paradigms and were tied to fringe factions. However, Modi insists that there is a clear understanding and distinction between the two. He selects cabinet colleagues and people around him who demonstrate the ability to build good trust based on good performance. Unlike many previous leaders, trust in Modi does not depend only on his personality but also on his ability and performance. Earning his trust requires good delivery and product development. In short, it follows a simple formula: "You're doing well and you've earned my trust." Another important measure they seem to use is consistency of delivery. Any management guru will tell you that if there is one word that can replace "good," it is "relationship." To achieve desired results, managers need to involve employees and create processes that motivate employees to achieve good results. When a person gains the trust of his boss, he will feel safe and motivated to work.

Trust is the result of reciprocity. People like Episode Hart are here not because of their location or organizational affiliation, but because of their intelligence and ability to express themselves. Even in the Prime Minister's Office, a hotbed of visceral emotions and interests since the early 20th century, Modi has relied on braggarts rather than autocrats. Many work in former NCO organizations but are highly educated. Honesty and passion.

For great change to occur in the world, leadership must be effective and leaders must have complete trust in their employees. Nelson Mandela, a leader in South Africa's anti-conflict struggle, is an example of a confident leader who dedicated his life to fighting for the freedom of millions of South Africans. His faith is evident in his courage and desire to do what is right. Mandela spent 27 years in prison, but his followers in the African National Congress (Mandela later served as president of the African National Congress from 1991 to 1997) continued to trust him and dedicate their faith to him. give. He is known for his strong character, reliability and confidence, which is also reflected in the way he manages his processes. Chapters Abuse Chapters Abuse Chapters Abuse Chapters Proving His Abilities Chapters His leadership abilities have earned him support and trust in his leadership. Episode 44 This man is proof of his ability. Jang He received support and trust from leadership. Talent. 44. Although he is a man, the truth is that he is also very loyal and evil, revealing his heart. page. Chapter Yes, he is warm and kind. Chapter He seems comfortable talking to everyone, including his rivals. A reflection of these characteristics can be seen in Narendra Modi. Likewise, Mandela was an image-conscious person, and it is said that he pursued high-quality clothes while maintaining a very confident attitude. A similar example is Modi's preference for high-quality kurtas specially made by his beloved darzis. Above all, Nelson Mandela was a man of principles. Despite government threats, forced imprisonment, and institutional discrimination, his supporters could always count on his strong will to continue his work. Prime Minister Modi must work towards the development of this the country and must be patient and secure the trust of the people to bring about the desired change. Most of the things we use today are the result of ideas. The basis of innovation is creativity. Everything new and useful is born from a unique perspective on events, situations and people. "Be Different" is the motto for youth , because it attracts the attention of young people, but most of the time we miss the real face of Creativity is simple and is the best. In , written as creative solutions, the simplest, most logical and creative solutions to our basic needs consist of looking back critically and rethinking, looking at the solutions from a critical perspective. It may be said that this is often not the case, and this may be true, but the seeds of creativity lie in the balance of imagination and insight. The world is innovating with new ideas, ideas and technologies, all based on finding new solutions to the same problems. Sometimes it is considered good if only a few people have it, but in fact it is possible for anyone to come up with creative ideas.

The problem is in attitude and thought. Many people never allow their mind to step outside of their comfort zone and so they end up taking the form of a well-behaved frog. People, especially managers, need to know that they need to be able to get rid of old ideas that don't work and think creatively. They need to become creative problem solvers to solve problems better. Narendra Modi understands creativity and is focused on leveraging creativity while creating and cultivating a culture that encourages creativity and innovation. Leaders know that creativity and innovation are the lifeblood of their organizations and are essential to protecting their brands. New ideas can lead to projects that are better than others. His campaign in the 2014 Indian elections is an example of this. In Modi's own words, "When I look back at the entire campaign, three words come to my mind: broad, innovative and exciting." In an unprecedented victory, even his critics agreed that this campaign was truly creative. 3D rallies, chai pe charchas and widespread use of social media make the movement a great story that generations of politicians have learned in hopes of following. But communication is not part of creativity. His policy and governance model for Gujarat was a brilliant idea that placed Gujarat at the forefront of India's progress. Not only is Modi himself creative, but he also believes that creativity should be fostered at all levels of government. In 2011, the Gujarat government launched a new urban rehabilitation programme. Recommended payment is 7,000 INR. If the city could build a large-scale administration and employ engineers, planners, managers, etc. If they can strike a balance, then they will receive development grants. Because time was short, the public came up with creative ideas to fill the gaps. They recruit talent from engineering, architecture and design colleges in Gujarat and provide internships and training. This intervenes in traditional bureaucratic processes and gives citizens the opportunity to participate in governance and create real-life impacts.

UNIC has even awarded a United Nations award for innovation to Gujarat's government. They stated, "An innovative scheme designed by the Chief Minister's Office, Government of Gujarat, has been chosen to receive a United Nations award for creativity and innovation in improving delivery, transparency, accountability and responsiveness in public service. The state-wide attention on grievances through the application of technology is an open, transparent system facilitating direct access by citizens, including meeting with their Chief Minister and Senior Administrative Officers. The Senior Administrative Officers are then held accountable for appropriate responses to citizens' grievances'."

Leaders like Modi search continually for ideas and programs that are better than the present ones and serve the purpose in the most elementary manner. Ever since he took over the coveted post of the Prime Minister of India, Modi has come up with ideas to implement his missions. On August 15, 2014, Modi delivered a speech on Independence Day, where he mentioned a new initiative called the "Make in India" programme. A few weeks later, on September 25, the much-anticipated programme was launched to a great reception. It is a first of its kind initiative aimed at transforming India into a global manufacturing powerhouse by way of getting investors, both local and foreign, to invest in India. Norms, policies and procedures for prospective investors were created in order to make investment in India more attractive. With impressive foresight, Modi is trying to bring out the talent in our country and make it visible around the globe. By identifying local leaders in innovation and technology, Modi would try to make them into global leaders,empowering and encouraging them in the process.

To make this initiative smooth and effective, Modi has set up systems. He has ensured guidance for investors at every step of the process by way of a separate unit of the Commerce Ministry called 'Invest India'; a dedicated cell and web portal to answer queries within 72 hours; easier regulations to attract investments in infrastructure, facilitating the 100 smart cities project, another creative and innovative venture proposed by Modi. The Make in India program also has further initiatives to foster innovation, protect intellectual property rights and creating better infrastructure as well as promoting state-of-the-art technology. Many people think that creativity is something that is hard to see and very different in many ways, but this may not be true. The "outside the box" vision often overlooks the importance of "good connections" with stakeholders. Gandhi captured the public imagination with simple things like salt during his Dandi March. Similarly, Modi captured the public imagination with his "Ache Din" speech by sending a simple message and without the noise of connection. The simple and vague lyrics of "Ache Din" may mean different things to different people, but they are very important for everyone.

Coming from the grassroots, Modi understands that India's technology and development often face challenges with unique characteristics. The previous NDA government fell due to 'Shining India' and tech is still seen as a big city. But it is creative to combine both to make a good impression. Modi's philosophy, like his vision, has a powerful back flow mechanism that captures people's ideas through a simple but unexpected system. Anyone in India can report pain during simple check proof. Although there is no legal justification, no one wants to touch the system that has been in existence since the British government. However, with a simple change in self-awareness (the model followed by the best administrations), Modi not only demonstrated the creativity of governance but also sent a strong message of creativity, making many of his rivals think about the place. Fans are wondering what he will do next. Modi used a good strategy to stay with all stakeholders. He approaches this as an ongoing process, not a one-off idea. There are very few examples in human history where creativity has been used as a tool for collective action. We can try to compare this to Barack Obama, who was born of change and hope but gradually showed his creativity.

Another important aspect of Modi's creativity defies the basic manner in which creativity is understood in normal parlance. Often creativity is attributed to a sudden streak of serendipity and thus its propagators state that it cannot be planned. Modi's model of creativity however has a strong base of planning and vision. He couples his grassroots knowledge and engagement with a fine understanding of simplifying governance entanglement. He presents ideas and systems which on face might sound simple when implemented, but nevertheless appear to people as new and novel. His model of creativity is thus more of re engineering that absolutely new (of which there is very little chance in India) yet they offer a creative paradigm to masses. Another example of Modi's creativity is displayed in his approach of connecting with different segments at large and using mediums which had lost out to newer media. His address to school kids across India on Children's day (a segment which has often remained ignored except for ceremonial connect, but holds a great potential as future target) or his addresses through All India Radio (a medium reaching to people who have yet to come in touch with the internet and others) urging the masses to send him ideas indeed has been great success, with PMO receiving 5000-6000 letters daily. These examples are not just simple but rechristen the creativity of governance. A decade ago when for the first time in India Modi's election campaign used a simple yet novel method of face masks of Modi, India saw another example of simple creativity. In his rallies people would wear simple paper masks having Modi's face and everyone would thus represent a reflection of Modi. His idea caught the fancy of his opponents and compatriots who wilfully followed his creativity and novel method.

While these examples of reaching to masses through simple yet ignored method, Modi introduced the Indian masses to completely high tech methods of 3-D animation. A person in a remote town or village could see a 3D Modi speaking to them and interacting with them; this was not just a technical marvel in itself but a direct connect and a method which was probably used for the first time in the world at such a large scale and with such sustenance.

However, what remains core to Modi's strategy of creativity is his constant desire to remain connected with the masses and electorate which has indeed borne great fruits for him. This is quite unlikely to his peers who generally tend to create a hollow circle around them limiting the access to the common people.

CHAPTER 17

The Legacy Of Narendra Modi

Personal insights into Narendra Modi's life

His hobbies, interests, and daily routines

Narendra Modi, born on September 17, 1950, in Vadnagar, a small town in the Indian state of Gujarat, is a prominent political figure known for his leadership in the Bharatiya Janata Party (BJP) and his tenure as the Prime Minister of India. Beyond his political career, there are intriguing aspects of his personal life and hobbies that provide a more holistic view of the man behind the office.

Modi's early life was marked by simplicity and determination. He belonged to a humble family, and his father, Damodardas, ran a tea stall, where a young Narendra helped his family by selling tea. His childhood was unpretentious, often spending time in the company of his books and helping his father. This modest upbringing instilled in him a strong work ethic and a deep connection to his roots.

As a young boy, Modi displayed an early interest in the Rashtriya Swayamsevak Sangh (RSS), a Hindu nationalist organization. This association laid the foundation for his later political career, where he emerged as a staunch proponent of Hindutva ideology.

Narendra Modi's personal life is characterized by a certain asceticism. He is known for his disciplined routine, which often begins with an early morning yoga session. Yoga holds a special place in his heart, and he has been an advocate for its physical and mental health benefits. His dedication to yoga is evident in his efforts to promote it on the global stage, including the declaration of International Day of Yoga by the United Nations in 2014.

Modi's dietary habits are also quite simple. He is a vegetarian and believes in the importance of a clean and healthy lifestyle. His meals are frugal and typically consist of simple vegetarian dishes. This lifestyle choice aligns with his belief in sustainable living and environmental conservation.

Beyond his political responsibilities, Narendra Modi has a few personal interests and hobbies. He is an avid reader and has often spoken about the importance of books in his life. Biographies and historical accounts intrigue him, and he enjoys reading to gain insights and knowledge.

Another prominent hobby of Modi is writing. He occasionally pens poems and articles, often reflecting on his experiences and perspectives. This creative outlet allows him to express his thoughts and emotions, offering a glimpse into his inner world.

Narendra Modi is also passionate about photography. He has a keen eye for capturing the beauty of landscapes and moments during his travels. His photographs often find their way onto his social media profiles, providing a more personal touch to his public image.

In his leisure time, Modi enjoys spending time in solitude, reflecting on his goals and strategies. He believes that moments of solitude are essential for self-improvement and personal growth.

Narendra Modi's personal life is a blend of simplicity, discipline, and a deep-rooted connection to his cultural heritage. His hobbies and interests, including yoga, reading, writing, and photography, reflect his multifaceted personality. While he is best known for his political achievements, his personal life and interests provide a more comprehensive understanding of the man who has played a pivotal role in shaping India's political landscape.

Criticisms and Controversies

Narendra Modi, India's 14th Prime Minister, has encountered a range of criticisms and controversies during his tenure. Here, we delve into ten of the most notable ones, along with his responses and their consequences.

Criticism 1: 2002 Gujarat Riots

Critics allege that Modi, as Chief Minister of Gujarat, did not take sufficient action to prevent or control the 2002 Gujarat riots, which resulted in significant loss of life, mainly among Muslims.

Response: Modi and his government maintain that they did everything within their power to contain the violence and bring stability to the state. The Supreme Court-appointed Special Investigation Team (SIT) did not find enough evidence to prosecute him.

Consequence: The controversy continues to haunt Modi, raising questions about his role during the riots and its implications for his political career.

Criticism 2: Demonetization

Demonetization in 2016, where high-denomination currency notes were invalidated, drew criticism for its suddenness and the disruptions it caused to the Indian economy and daily life.

Response: Modi defended demonetization as a necessary step to combat corruption, black money, and counterfeit currency. He claimed it would transition India towards a digital economy.

Consequence: While some supported the move, there were economic disruptions and hardships for many citizens. Its long-term impact remains a subject of debate.

Criticism 3: Handling of the COVID-19 Pandemic

Modi's government faced criticism for its handling of the COVID-19 pandemic, including the sudden nationwide lockdown, which caused distress among migrant workers and strained healthcare resources.

Response: The government increased healthcare infrastructure and initiated vaccination drives. Modi urged unity and adherence to safety measures.

Consequence: The consequences of India's response to the pandemic are still being evaluated, with debates about its effectiveness and the hardships endured during the lockdown.

Criticism 4: Freedom of Press and Dissent

Concerns have risen about restrictions on freedom of the press and the intimidation faced by journalists and critics under Modi's government.

Response: The government maintains it respects freedom of expression but emphasizes responsible journalism.

Consequence: Debates persist about the state of democracy and freedom of expression in India, with allegations of a chilling effect on dissent.

Criticism 5: Economic Slowdown

Critics argue that India experienced an economic slowdown during Modi's tenure, raising concerns about job creation and economic reforms.

Response: The government has introduced various economic reforms and initiatives to boost growth.

Consequence: Economic performance and job creation continue to be subjects of scrutiny and debate.

Criticism 6: Agrarian Distress

Protests by farmers against agricultural reforms have led to criticism of the government's handling of agrarian issues.

Response: The government has engaged in dialogues with farmers to address their concerns and has offered amendments to the contentious laws.

Consequence: The farmers' protests continue, highlighting the complexities of agrarian policy reform.

Criticism 7: Social Divisions

Critics allege that Modi's leadership has exacerbated social and religious divisions in India.

Response: The government has emphasized unity and inclusivity, with Modi often calling for 'Sabka Saath, Sabka Vikas' (Together with all, Development for all).

Consequence: Debates persist on the impact of divisive rhetoric on social cohesion.

Criticism 8: Human Rights

Concerns have been raised about human rights issues, including alleged extrajudicial encounters and restrictions in conflict regions like Kashmir.

Response: The government maintains its actions are necessary for national security.

Consequence: Human rights concerns continue to be a contentious issue, with calls for transparency and accountability.

Criticism 9: Nationalism Debate

The government's emphasis on nationalism and its impact on dissent and diversity have sparked debates on pluralism and inclusivity.

Response: The government argues that a strong national identity is essential for a unified and progressive India.

Consequence: Debates on the balance between nationalism and diversity persist.

Criticism 10: Environmental Policies

Critics question the government's approach to environmental conservation and climate change, particularly concerning industrial development projects.

Response: The government claims it is balancing development and environmental conservation.

Consequence: Environmental concerns remain a topic of debate, especially in projects affecting ecologically sensitive areas.

These criticisms and controversies have contributed to the complex and evolving narrative of Narendra Modi's leadership, with consequences that continue to shape India's political landscape and public discourse.

Narendra Modi, a significant figure in Indian politics, has left a lasting impact on India's political landscape. Here's a detailed look at his influence:

1. **Humble Origins:** Narendra Modi was born on September 17, 1950, in Vadnagar, Gujarat, and grew up in modest circumstances.
2. **RSS and Early Years:** He joined the Rashtriya

Swayamsevak Sangh (RSS) in his youth, where he imbibed the principles of Hindutva and began his political journey.

3. **Rise in Gujarat:** Modi's early political career saw him serving in the state of Gujarat. He became its Chief Minister in 2001.

4. **Economic Development:** Under his leadership, Gujarat experienced significant economic growth and development, earning him the nickname "Gujarat's development man."

5. **2002 Gujarat Riots:** However, his tenure was also marred by controversy, particularly the 2002 Gujarat riots, which raised questions about his role during the violence.

6. **National Stage:** In 2014, Narendra Modi led the Bharatiya Janata Party (BJP) to a historic victory in the general elections.

7. **Prime Ministerial Tenure:** Modi became India's 14th Prime Minister, and his impact on India's political landscape began to take shape.

8. **Flagship Initiatives:** He launched flagship initiatives like "Make in India" and "Digital India" to boost manufacturing and digitization.

9. **Swachh Bharat Abhiyan:** His "Swachh Bharat Abhiyan" aimed at promoting cleanliness and sanitation across India.

10. **Foreign Policy:** Modi's foreign policy focused on strengthening ties with key nations, including the United States and neighboring countries.

11. **Climate Change:** He played a significant role in

the global fight against climate change, particularly through the International Solar Alliance.

12. **Economic Reforms:** Modi's government introduced the "Goods and Services Tax" (GST) and initiated demonetization to curb black money.

13. **Social Welfare:** Initiatives like "Ayushman Bharat" aimed at providing health insurance to millions of underprivileged Indians.

14. **Infrastructure Development:** Under his leadership, India witnessed advancements in infrastructure development, including roads and highways.

15. **Nationalism:** Modi's leadership emphasized strong nationalism, shaping India's political discourse.

16. **Criticism and Controversy:** His government faced criticism for alleged restrictions on freedom of expression and dissent.

17. **Defense Modernization:** Modi continued to prioritize India's defense capabilities and modernization of the armed forces.

18. **Gender Equality:** Initiatives like "Beti Bachao, Beti Padhao" promoted gender equality and female education.

19. **COVID-19 Response:** His leadership played a crucial role in India's response to the COVID-19 pandemic.

20. **Self-Reliance:** "Atmanirbhar Bharat" emphasized self-reliance and reducing dependency on imports.

21. **Global Influence:** Modi's foreign visits and diplomacy enhanced India's global standing and influence.

22. **Communication Skills:** His charisma and communication skills made him a prominent global leader.

23. **Re-election:** He won re-election in 2019 with a resounding mandate, solidifying his impact on Indian politics.

24. **BJP Expansion:** The BJP expanded its influence across various states under Modi's leadership.

25. **Economic Policy:** The concept of "One Nation, One Tax" was realized through the GST.

26. **Cultural Emphasis:** His leadership saw a renewed on traditional Indian culture and values.

27. **Digital Governance:** Initiatives like "Digital India" aimed at making government services accessible online.

28. **Renewable Energy:** Modi promoted renewable energy and environmental conservation, advancing India's sustainability efforts.

29. **Yoga Promotion:** He promoted yoga on the international stage, leading to the declaration of International Day of Yoga by the United Nations.

30. **Promoting Local Businesses:** The "Vocal for Local" campaign aimed at promoting local businesses and products.

Narendra Modi's impact on India and its political landscape has been both transformative and divisive, making him a central figure in the nation's political history. His legacy continues to shape India's future while facing both praise and criticism.

The potential future implications of his leadership:

1. **Economic Development:** Narendra Modi's leadership has emphasized economic growth and development. His policies such as "Make in India" and "Digital India" have aimed at boosting manufacturing and technology sectors. In the future, this could result in sustained economic growth, job creation, and increased foreign investments. However, there will be challenges in ensuring that this growth benefits all segments of the population, including marginalized communities.

2. **Geopolitical Influence:** Under Modi's leadership, India has sought to strengthen its position in global politics. The "Act East Policy" has focused on enhancing India's relations with countries in East and Southeast Asia. The future implications include a more assertive Indian role in international affairs, particularly in South Asia and relations with major powers like the United States, China, and Russia. Managing these relationships will be critical to India's geopolitical standing.

3. **Social and Cultural Dynamics:** Modi's leadership has sparked debates about the intersection of religion and politics in India. His affiliation with the Rashtriya Swayamsevak Sangh (RSS) and the Bharatiya Janata Party (BJP), which have roots in Hindu nationalism, has raised questions about secularism and religious diversity in India. In the future, there may be continued discussions and potential societal shifts in how religion and politics interact, with implications for India's social fabric.

4. **Environmental Sustainability:** India faces significant environmental challenges, including air pollution, water scarcity, and climate change. Modi's leadership will be crucial in determining how

India addresses these issues. Future implications may involve adopting cleaner energy sources, implementing stricter environmental regulations, and promoting sustainable practices. Balancing economic development with environmental protection will be a key challenge.

5. **Infrastructure and Connectivity:** Modi's leadership has introduced ambitious infrastructure projects such as "Smart Cities" and the "Bullet Train." These initiatives aim to transform India's transportation, urban planning, and connectivity. In the future, improved infrastructure can enhance the quality of life for citizens, promote economic development, and create jobs. However, ensuring equitable access to these developments across regions and communities will be essential to avoid growing disparities.

6. **Healthcare and Education:** The COVID-19 pandemic highlighted the importance of healthcare infrastructure and access to quality education. Modi's leadership will likely play a significant role in shaping the future of healthcare and education in India. Investments in healthcare systems, expansion of digital education, and improving the quality of healthcare and education services will have long-term implications for the well-being and future prospects of India's population.

7. **Digital Transformation:** Modi's focus on digitalization, evident in initiatives like "Digital India," can lead to greater access to technology and online services for millions of Indians. This can revolutionize various sectors, including finance, education, and healthcare. However, ensuring digital inclusivity and addressing cybersecurity challenges will be important for the future.

8. **Defense and National Security:** Modi's leadership has seen a focus on modernizing India's defense forces and enhancing its national security capabilities. In the future, this could lead to a stronger and more secure India, potentially impacting regional stability and India's ability to address security challenges effectively.

9. **Foreign Policy and Diplomacy:** Modi's foreign policy has emphasized strengthening relations with neighboring countries and fostering strategic partnerships globally. Future implications may include India playing a more prominent role in international organizations, such as the United Nations, and participating in global initiatives related to climate change, peacekeeping, and humanitarian efforts.

10. **Agriculture and Rural Development:** Agriculture remains a significant part of India's economy, and Modi's leadership has introduced reforms aimed at modernizing this sector. In the future, these reforms could lead to increased agricultural productivity, income for farmers, and rural development. However, ensuring that small and marginalized farmers benefit from these changes will be crucial.

11. **Social Welfare Programs:** Modi's government has launched various social welfare programs like "Pradhan Mantri Jan Dhan Yojana" and "Swachh Bharat Abhiyan." These programs aim to address poverty, sanitation, and financial inclusion. In the future, they may have long-term implications for poverty reduction, healthcare access, and sanitation improvements, especially in rural areas.

12. **Innovation and Start-up Ecosystem:** Under Modi's leadership, India has witnessed the growth

of its start-up ecosystem and investments in research and development. The future implications include a thriving innovation economy, with Indian start-ups making significant contributions to technology, healthcare, and other industries, both domestically and internationally.

13. **Cultural and Soft Power Influence:** India's cultural and soft power, including Bollywood, yoga, and Indian cuisine, have gained global recognition. Modi's leadership can further harness these elements to promote Indian culture and heritage worldwide. This can lead to increased tourism, trade, and international partnerships.

14. **Social Harmony and Inclusivity:** Promoting social harmony and inclusivity is essential for a diverse country like India. Modi's leadership will play a role in fostering unity among various communities. The future implications involve efforts to bridge cultural and religious divides, promoting tolerance, and ensuring equal opportunities for all citizens.

15. **Regional Development:** Balancing development across different states and regions of India is a significant challenge. Modi's leadership may focus on reducing regional disparities by investing in infrastructure, education, and healthcare in less developed areas, which could lead to more equitable growth.

In summary, Narendra Modi's leadership has multifaceted implications for India's future. These encompass defense and security, foreign policy, agriculture, social welfare, innovation, cultural influence, social harmony, regional development, and more. As India navigates the complex challenges of the 21st century, Modi's leadership will continue to shape the nation's path and influence its role on the global stage. The successful implementation of policies in these areas will be critical for India's long-term progress and development.

CHAPTER 18

"Strategic Moves: Modi's Visionary Initiatives for National Development and Governance"

PM Modi's strategy focuses on Reform, Perform and Transform and encompasses engaging with different segments of the population, identifying the right man at the right place at the right time, economic reforms, banking reforms, capacity building in the social sector, work on financial and digital inclusion, the pursuit of saturation in basic necessities such as sanitation, electricity and housing, and unprecedented investment in infrastructure. I have analyzed PM Modi's strategy in five sections in this chapter: Section 1 Strategies about connecting with different segmentation of Populations like military, women, farmers, the poor, and the underprivileged, Students, Teachers, Parents, Indian Diaspora, and Sports Persons etc. Section 2 Identifying Star Performers in Key Roles Section 3 Strategies about building "Brand India" through some world-class projects like the world's biggest sports stadium, the world's tallest statue, the world's largest meetings, convention and exhibition destination etc.

Section 4 Some other Key Strategies including economic, defence, Foreign Policy etc. Section 5 Political Maneuvering Section 1 Connecting with some key segments of Population Connecting with People Man, Ki Bat: Mann Ki Baat is a monthly radio programme in which Modi shares his thoughts on a range of issues. Launched in 2014, the programme has been broadcast in 24 languages and has a listenership of over 30 million. "In the 100th episode of "Mann Ki Baat", PM Modi credited his monthly radio broadcast for allowing him to stay connected with people without the impediments of protocol and security. He said that it had become a catalyst for social causes. "Every month I witnessed brilliant aspects of my countrymen. One after the other, I witnessed the pinnacle of hard work and dedication. I never feel that I am even slightly away from you. For me, this is not just a programme, rather it is faith, worship and resolve. Just as people worship deities by offering prasad, for me, Mann Ki Baat is that offering at the feet of my countrymen...He said. The PM also acknowledged the publicity his show has garnered across the globe. The 100th episode was aired live at the United Nations headquarters.

Narendra Modi App: Another strategy of Modi to remain connected with people is creating Narendra Modi App which has a record of the most downloaded political app in the world. The app is one of the most technologically savvy apps. This is an app that Prime Minister Modi follows himself, not just once but many times daily, to keep track of what people are saying or thinking. Through App, PM Modi gets a pulse of the nation and ideas from people who can contribute to India's story. It also facilitates to seek suggestions on policy issues. And many times, the Prime Minister himself responds to a person whose idea or comment he likes. The app gives one the power to associate with many of the Prime Minister's initiatives – like volunteering for Swachh Bharat or associating with Digital India or My Gov. To list just a few examples: Lakhs of citizens sent their birthday wishes to Prime Minister Modi via the Narendra Modi App. Thousands of people took the Swachh Bharat pledge on 2nd October. Connecting with Army From 2014 onwards, since the last 9 years, Modi has spent every Diwali with soldiers to bring some joy to the lives of the armed forces personnel posted at some of the remotest security check posts. "Diwali is a festival we celebrate with family, and with those, we call our own. So each year I spend time with you all because you all are my own, my family. I bring sweets for you all today. But these are not just from me. It is from all 130 crore Indians." Modi keeps saying to soldiers. Connecting with women "Women are emerging as the driving force of our growth journey. Many development initiatives are seeing them come to the forefront, be it financial inclusion, entrepreneurship or cleanliness. With the G20, now, the message of women-led development is making waves all over the world – this is the power of Indian women," the PM said during the Money control interview in September 2023. Let's delve a little bit further into each initiative with regard to connecting with women. Abolishing the Triple Talaq One of the most significant political achievements of the Modi government in its second term in office has been the passage of the triple talaq bill in Parliament, a law that made instant triple talaq a criminal offence. The triple talaq law, formally called the Muslim Women (Protection of Rights on Marriage) Act, 2019, was passed on August 1, 2019, after intense debates in Parliament. By abolishing the Triple Talaq, the Modi Government has strengthened the socio-economic, fundamental and constitutional rights of Muslim women. Women Reservation Nari Shakti Vandan Adhiniyam (Constitution (128th Amendment) Bill,2023 A new bill named "Nari Shakti Vandan Adhiniyam (Constitution (128th)

Amendment) Bill,2023 to reserve 33% seats in Lok Sabha, state assemblies and the legislative assembly of the NCT of Delhi for women was introduced in the Parliament on 19/9/23 which was passed in Lok Sabha on 20/9/23 and Rajya Sabaha on 21/9/23. Reservation will be applicable after the delimitation that will happen after the census. Such reservation exists already at the lowest tiers of government in Panchayat Raj institutions. So many women parliamentarians and legislators in elective offices will be a force for good. Increase in Maternity leave Another significant step taken was Increasing paid maternity leave period from 12 weeks to 26 weeks which makes work-life balance possible for working women. Ujjawala Scheme The Pradhan Mantri Ujjwala Yojana was launched by the Modi regime in 2016 to distribute 500 lakh LPG connections to women of Below Poverty Line (BPL) families.

The free LPG connection scheme, popularly known as Ujjwala has empowered women, giving them relief from the dust and fumes of the traditional chulhas. It is only because of his appeal that crores of people voluntarily surrendered the subsidies that they were availing on their LPG connections. In September 2023, the Government decided to increase the total number of Ujjwala beneficiaries by giving out 75 lakh new connections, taking their total strength to 10.35 crore. Beti Bachao, Beti Padhao (Save Girl, Educate Girl) Through the Beti Bachao, Beti Padhao campaign, Modi exposed the evils of Indian society and advised people to treat their daughters at par with their sons by giving them respect, love, education and rights. Notable progress has also been made in the education of women. Sukanya Samriddhi Yojana, launched as part of 'Beti Bachao Beti Padhao', to facilitate the education of the girl child, has already reached out to more than three crore aspirational young women. Further, there has been encouraging progress on the front of women's higher education as well. For instance, there has been an increase in PhD enrolment of women to 43.82 per cent in 2018 from 40 per cent in 2013-14 because of various measures taken by the government, such as women candidates being allowed a relaxation of one year for M.Phil. and two years for PhD in the maximum duration, i.e. two to six years respectively as per the University Grants Commission (UGC), in 2016. Pradhan Mantri Matru Vandana Yojana (PMMVY) To promote women-led development, a key focus has been on building capacities in terms of nutrition, health, and education. In 2017, the government launched the Pradhan Mantri Matru Vandana Yojana (PMMVY), a direct benefit transfer (DBT) for pregnant women and lactating mothers to meet enhanced nutritional needs and to partially compensate for wage loss. In FY 2019-20, the scheme has crossed a significant milestone by reaching out to one crore beneficiaries. Likewise, there have been remarkable improvements in women's health and access to sanitation. Under Swatch Bharat Mission-Gramin, there has been a rapid increase in target achievement from

39 per cent in 2014 to 100 per cent in 2019 with more than 10 crore toilets built since 2014. The impact of such infrastructural developments is corroborated by a UNICEF study on 'Access to Toilets and Safety, Convenience and Self-respect of Women in Rural India' (February 2020), which states that 91 per cent of the women reported that they have been able to save up to an hour and do not have to travel up to a kilometer for defecation after the construction of toilets. Further, the decline in the maternal mortality rate from 167 (in 2011-13) to 113 (in 2016-18) exemplifies the government's commitment to promoting maternal health and well-being.

Connecting with India's Young Generation PM Modi has famously said, "The world has admitted that India has two limitless powers – demography & democracy." India currently has the world's largest young population, and PM Modi is focusing on harnessing its potential to the fullest. The National Education Policy (NEP) of 2020 overhauled the existing education system after over thirty years. NEP envisions a paradigm shift in the Indian school and higher education system that is rooted in Indian ethos, is more learner-centric, and aims to make India a global knowledge superpower. In the last nine years alone, a record number of new IITs, IIMs, medical colleges, and universities have been opened across the country.

Along with education, skilling, and up skilling has also been the focus of the Modi government. Since its launch, more than 1.37 crore youngsters have received skill training under the PM Kaushal Vikas Yojana, thereby improving their employment prospects. Consistent efforts to transform India into an attractive investment hub, assisting MSMEs and programmes such as the Production Linked Incentive Scheme for domestic production have contributed towards creating employment opportunities for young Indians. The youth are also being allowed to serve in the Armed Forces under the Agnipath scheme. The focus has not been just to create employment but also to build entrepreneurship, transforming the youth from job seekers to job creators. Unlike earlier when people were risk averse and opted for salaried jobs, the youth today are raring to go because of the conducive policy environment. Through the Startup India programme that was launched in 2016, the Modi government has taken numerous measures to promote entrepreneurship by providing a host of tax benefits, easing regulations and reducing the compliance burden. Like entrepreneurship, sports were considered a distraction for most young people, and they were discouraged from pursuing it professionally.

However, PM Modi brought a crucial behavioral and mindset change and introduced various policies that have allowed innumerable youngsters to fulfill their dream of pursuing sports a career. India saw it's best-ever performance in history during the Tokyo Olympics and Paralympics in 2021. This has been an outcome of long-term planning and support through the flagship Target Olympic Podium Scheme. As India enters Amrit Kaal, its demographic dividend is uniquely poised to usher in an era of rapid social, economic, and technological innovation and advancement. Connecting with Farmers In –9year, PM Modi introduced 9 welfare schemes for farmers. From Pradhan Mantri Fasal Bima Yojana (PMFBY) to Pradhan Mantri Kisan Samman Nidhi (PMKSN), the Narendra Modi Government has introduced numerous initiatives aimed at transforming the agricultural sector and empowering farmers across the country. Under PM Modi's leadership, these initiatives have aimed to improve the lives of farmers by providing financial security, skill development, market access, and sustainable agricultural practices.

Via the Pradhan Mantri Kisan Samman Nidhi PM KISAN) scheme, launched in 2019, the government has been giving farmers Rs 6,000 per year as minimum income support. Some other notable schemes are the Soil Health Card Scheme, Pradhan Mantri Kaushal Vikas Yojana (PMKVY), e-NAM (National Agriculture Market), Pradhan Mantri Atmanirbhar Bharat Abhiyan (ABHA). Paramparagat Krishi Vikas Yojana (PKVY), Pradhan Mantri Krishi Sinchai Yojana (PMKSY), PM Krishi Sampada Yojana etc. These are just a few of the many schemes and initiatives that PM Modi has introduced to improve the lives of farmers and the agriculture sector in India. These schemes have helped to improve the income of farmers, reduce their financial burden, and make the agriculture sector more sustainable. Connecting with Poor and underprivileged Population Bringing Prosperity to Poor Serving the poor and the marginalized has been the underlying premise of the Modi government, a promise that is guided by the principle of 'Antyodaya' which means that the goal of development isn't complete till it reaches the last person in society. Let's delve a little bit further into each initiative for connecting with Poor and Underprivileged. Campaign for toilets Earlier, 60 per cent of the country's village homes didn't have toilets for generations. The majority of them didn't have it because of poverty, but a few didn't because of ill beliefs prevalent among them despite their prosperity. The major sufferers were women who had to face physical as well as mental torture because of the absence of toilets in the house. Modi did it smartly, working on two fronts. First, the Government sanctioned a grant to such poor people who were unable to make toilets due to the lack of funds and water. Secondly, he took upon the task of enlightening such people who refrained from making toilets due to their ill-conceived belief systems through his campaigns. He appealed to the women to pressure their menfolk to provide toilets in their homes. The trick worked, and today one could gauge the success of Swachh Bharat Mission with more than 95 per cent of households having toilets in comparison with 2014's figure of 40 per cent.

Health insurance Ayushman Bharat: Ayushman Bharat is

a National Health Protection Scheme, which will cover over 10 crore poor and vulnerable families (approximately 50 crore beneficiaries) providing coverage of up to 5 lakh rupees per family per year for secondary and tertiary care hospitalization.

Mudra, Stand UP India MUDRA Yojana and Stand-Up India are creating a large pool of young entrepreneurs from marginalized groups. More than half of the 40 crore loans given under MUDRA have been given to SC/ST/OBC entrepreneurs. This is ushering in empowerment of not just individuals but is also a means to empower the traditionally neglected communities. Reservation to Economically Weaker Section Modi government's historic decision to provide reservations for economically weaker sections provided much-needed support to poor households. PM Vishwakarma On 19th September 2023, on the 73rd Birthday of PM Modi which coincides with Vishwakarma Jayanti, PM Modi launched an ambitious scheme "PM Vishwakarma" which is aimed at helping artisans, craftsmen and others engaged in traditional skills. The outlay of the scheme is Rs. 13,000 crores. Since practitioners of these traditional occupations come largely from Other Backward Classes (OBC), the scheme will benefit this politically important segment. Under the Scheme, eligible persons will get loans up to Rs.3 lacs without any security with an interest rate of only 5 %. They will also be provided training for skill upgradation with Rs.500 as a stipend per day. Help will also be provided for quality certifi certification, branding and marketing of their products. Connecting with Sports Persons One of the biggest factors in the tectonic shift in the attitude of politicians and bureaucrats towards sports persons has been Prime Minister Narendra Modi's focus on making sports persons heroes of today's India. From Mirabai Chanu to the Thomas Cup winners to the thousands of sports persons who have raised the tricolor in the international arena, Modi has invariably been the first to lead in appreciating and congratulatory messages. This amplifies the accomplishments as apart from the staggering buzz on social media, the news is picked up across media outlets, and the athlete and the sport enjoy the spotlight. The sports person gains instant recognition, becomes a celebrity, and this leads to much-needed sponsors and funding. This has been backed by the government undertaking remarkable changes at the grassroots level across sporting disciplines where there has been a massive infrastructure improvement. Connecting with Students, Teachers and Parents PM Modi had been actively engaging with students through events like "Pariksha Pe Charcha" (a discussion on exams) and other initiatives. Modi's interaction with students through "Pariksha Pe Charcha" is an annual event where he would address students, parents, and teachers, offering them guidance and encouragement during exam seasons. These interactions were designed to reduce stress and anxiety among students and motivate them to excel in their studies. Connecting with Indian diaspora PM Modi has often addressed gatherings of the Indian diaspora during his foreign visits. These events are usually attended by people of Indian origin who live in the host country. He uses these occasions to share updates on India's progress and to strengthen ties between the diaspora and their home country. He also has attended and addressed the Pravasi Bharatiya Divas; an annual event organized by the Government of India to engage with the Indian diaspora. It provides a platform for discussions on various issues affecting PIOs and NRIs. During his visits, Modi has often interacted with business and tech leaders of Indian origin, encouraging them to invest in India and contribute to its development. He has promoted initiatives like "Make in India" and "Digital India" to attract investments. PM Modi has participated in cultural and religious events organized by the Indian diaspora, such as visiting temples, gurudwaras, and other places of worship. These visits help connect with the cultural and spiritual aspects of the Indian community abroad. The Indian government has initiated several programs to facilitate engagement with the diaspora. One notable example is the Overseas Citizenship of India (OCI) card, which allows people of Indian origin to enjoy certain privileges in India, such as travel and residence. Padma Prizes PM Modi brought the credibility of prestigious Padma awards back. Modi gave it to the average person and restored the glory that was once associated with it. To fill such positions, the administration began its selection process at the grassroots level by seeking persons who had served the masses and were among the commoners. The honorees were individuals who never made headlines in newspapers or news outlets; rather, they were the people who worked selflessly for the public. Section 2 Identifying Star Performers in Key Roles Without the help of a strong, committed, capable team, a leader cannot accomplish significant results. Leadership Mastery lies in the right man at the right place at the right time. PM Modi's identification of certain key roles is extraordinary. For example, bringing in former Foreign Secretary S. Jaishankar as his Minister for External Affairs was his master stroke. S. Jaishankar, a career diplomat, brought extensive experience in foreign affairs to his role as the Minister of External Affairs. Modi has shown enormous dexterity for a politician whose natural inclination would have been to have a fellow politician, preferably a loyalist, in the South Block, toeing the line. Unencumbered by the compulsions of politics, Modi chose Jaishankar for his professional abilities and today everyone can see how well he has performed during the last four years. Another interesting identification was that of Ajit Kumar Doval as National Security Advisor of India. Ajit Doval, with his background in intelligence and security, was well-suited for his role as the National Security Advisor. The identification of Amit Shah initially as a President of Party and later as a Home Minister was another master selection. Amit Shah, called the "Chanakya" of modern day Indian politics provided great support to Modi in all his endeavors.

Amit Shah built the party's campaign systematically around the nationalism plank and the Prime Minister's popularity.

The identification of Yogi Adityanath as Chief Minister for UP is an another powerful selection. From the day he was appointed as CM of Uttar Pradesh, he never sat for relief and refreshments. Take a look at several contributions made by Yogi Adityanath that show he has successfully reformed the state with good governance. Adityanath has become the first CM in 70 years of UP's electoral history to complete a full tenure of five years and go on to win a second consecutive term. One more interesting selection was that of Amitabh Kant as Sherpa of G 20. An alumnus of St Stephen's College and Jawaharlal Nehru University, Kant has been Modi's 'go-to-guy' for almost a decade. When Modi was sworn in as Prime Minister on May 26, 2014, Kant was serving as secretary in the Department of Industrial Policy & Promotion. Although it was a low-profile department, Kant emerged as a key person in the bureaucracy, driving Modi's pet projects like Ease of Doing Business, Make-in-India and Start-up India. Barely a week after demitting the office of Niti Aayog, Kant was appointed G20 Sherpa. During the G20 Summit in Delhi in September 2023, there was a huge divide between the member countries on the Russia-Ukraine issue. The US, the UK and Germany wanted to strongly condemn the Russian war against Ukraine, while on the other side; China and Russia were insisting that there should be no mention of the subject. But India not only managed to bridge this gulf but also forged a 100% consensus. Terming it a historic achievement, Kant said, "This is the first time that all 83 paras have 100% consensus." This again proves the master identification of Amitabh Kant as G20 Sherpa by PM Modi. Section 3 Building "Brand India" by world-class Projects India's largest-ever Exhibition and Convention Center "YashoBhoomi" India International Convention and Expo Center (IICC) named Yasho Bhoomi in Dwarka, New Delhi. (The first phase inauguration happened on 17/9/23).

It is among the world's largest meetings, convention and exhibition destinations with 8.9 lakh sq. Meter Project area. It includes one of the world's biggest exhibition halls, with each hall equivalent to 5 football fields. It will have underground parking for over 3,000 cars. It will be an IGBC platinum-certified structure with solar panels and a modern wastewater treatment system. The Convention Center will have a seating capacity of 11,000 delegates. It is equipped with India's largest LED media facade. World's largest Stadium Narendra Modi Stadium at Motera, Ahmedabad is the world's largest stadium with a seating capacity of 1,32,000. The field size of the stadium is 180 yards by 150 yards, and it spans 63 acres. 3,000 cars and 10,000 two-wheelers (like scooters or bikes) can park in the surrounding 18 parking zones around the stadium. There is also a cricket academy which can house 40 athletes within the stadium dormitory. World's biggest Solar Wind Park The Bhadla Solar Park is a solar power plant located in the Thar Desert of Rajasthan, India. It covers an area of 56 square kilometers and has a total installed capacity of 2,245 megawatts (MW), making it the largest solar park in the world as of 2023. World's tallest Rail Bridge The Chenab Bridge is the world's tallest railway bridge, standing at a height of 359 meters (1,178 feet) above the Chenab River. It's taller than both the Eiffel Tower in Paris and the Statue of Liberty in New York City. The bridge is located in Jammu and Kashmir is a part of the Udhampur-Srinagar-Baramulla Rail Link project.

For Prime Minister Narendra Modi, investments in infrastructure like the Chenab Bridge and the broader rail link project are seen as a powerful tool for social integration and political influence, connecting disparate regions with key cities something that has been sorely missing in India. World's tallest statue Statue of Unity The world's tallest statue, Statue of Unity, with a height of 182 meters (597 feet) has been created as a tribute to the 'Iron Man of India', Sardar Vallabhbhai Patel. It is located near Kevadia in the state of Gujarat, India. It depicts Indian statesman and independence activist Vallabhbhai Patel (1875–1950), who was the first deputy prime minister and home minister of independent India and an adherent of Mahatma Gandhi. Patel is highly respected for his leadership in uniting the 562 princely states of India to form the single Union of India. World's highest Motorable road -Umling La Pass The highest motorable road in the world is now in India. It is called the Umling La Pass and has been constructed by the Border Roads Organization (BRO) at a height of 19,300 feet. World's longest tunnel at a height of 10,000 feet Atal Tunnel On October 3, 2020, PM Narendra Modi inaugurated the Atal Tunnel, dedicating it to the nation. Spanning across a length of 9.02 km, the Atal Tunnel is strategically important, and it runs under the Rohtang Pass. It was built on the Manali – Leh Highway and the construction took place in freezing temperatures and very difficult terrain, making the task highly daunting. Now, the tunnel has been authentically certified as the longest one at such an altitude by the UK-based World of Records. Gift city -the new epicentre of Global Finance and IT "The vision is to create world class finance and IT zone for India to provide services not only to India but to entire world." PM Modi Gujarat International Finance Tec-City is a central business district in Gandhinagar district in Gujarat, India. It is India's first operational green field smart city and international financial services centre, which the Government of Gujarat promoted as a green field project. Prime Minister Modi conceptualised the project in 2008, as Chief Minister of Gujarat. GIFT City presents an unprecedented ecosystem for crucial economic activities with globally benchmarked regulations, taxation, policies and more, sup supported by Govt. Of India and Gujarat. The city mainly comprises of banks, capital market entities, insurance companies and captive manufacturing units. New Parliament house During the momentous 75th year of Independence, Narendra Modi, the Prime Minister of India, unveiled the new Parliament building. This architectural masterpiece was designed by Indian talent Bimal Patel. It embodies the entire nation's rich culture, pride, and spirit. The need for a new Indian Parliament building was long overdue.

According to government data, the old Parliament building of India, constructed in 1927, was not intended to accommodate a bicameral legislature. The seating arrangements thus became cramped and inconvenient. The new Indian Parliament building has a triangular layout covering approximately 65,000 sq metres. Key features of the New Parliament Building:

1. **Expanded seating capacity:** The new complex will have larger legislative chambers. Based on India's national bird peacock, the new Lok Sabha will have seating capacity at 888 seats, while there will be 348 seats for Rajya Sabha, which is based on the Lotus theme – the national flower. As per the new floor plan, the Lok Sabha hall will be able to accommodate 1,272 seats for joint sessions.

2. **The Shilp Deergha gallery** conceptualised around eight themes, showcases approximately 255 crafts sourced from around 400 artisans across India.

3. **Sengol:** At the inauguration of the new Parliament House, PM Modi established the historical and sacred "Sengol" in the Parliament House. This sacred "Sengol" is the symbol of the transfer of power from the British to India.

4. **The state-of-the-art 'Constitutional Hall'** – a new addition to the Parliament complex symbolically and physically puts the citizens "at the heart of the democracy," the Central Vista project website states.

5. **In the new complex,** the offices have been designed in an 'ultra-modern' fashion, geared with the latest communication technologies and are extremely secure and efficient. Additionally, the new complex will have larger committee rooms, equipped with the latest technology and purpose-design spaces to enhance efficiency. It also carries a thoughtfully designed library to give a "superior experience", equipped to serve the members with the relevant information.

6. **With a focus on energy efficiency,** the new complex is a "platinum-rated green building" and showcases India's "commitment towards sustainable development." It will also host many regional artworks to promote the diverse cultural heritage of the country.

7. **To promote inclusivity,** the new Parliament complex is also 'divyang-friendly'. It also features a central lounge to complement the open courtyard and is meant for members to interact. The open courtyard has the national tree 'Banyan' as well.

The existing building served as independent India's first Parliament and Witnessed the adoption of the Constitution of India. Thus, conserving and Rejuvenating the rich heritage of the Parliament building is a matter of national importance. Hence the Prime Minister announced the new name of The old parliament building which will Be called "Samvidhan Sadan" (Constitution House).

Bharat Mandapam

Covering an approximate campus area of 123 acres, Bharat Mandapam has been developed as India's largest MICE (Meetings, Incentives, Conferences, and Exhibitions) destination. Regarding the covered space available for events, this complex ranks among the top exhibition and convention complexes globally.

The architectural design of the Bharat Mandapam building draws inspiration from "India's rich traditions", symbolising the nation's confidence in its heritage while embracing modern amenities and contemporary living.

Bharat Mandapam offers a wealth of amenities, including numerous meeting rooms, lounges, auditoriums, an amphitheatre, and a fully-equipped business centre, enabling it to accommodate a wide spectrum of events. A 27-ft-tall bronze statue of Nataraja, made of Ashtadhatu and weighing about 18 tons, is installed at Bharat Mandapam.

G20 meeting was held in this Centre in September, 23 featuring top world leaders, including US President Joe Biden and UK Prime Minister Rishi Sunak.

Section 4 Some other Key Strategies including economic, defence, Foreign Policy etc:

1. Implementation of One Nation, one tax and thereby creating an open market for each state. GST was introduced

by abolishing Central Sales Tax, State-level sales tax, entry tax, stamp duty, telecom license fees, turnover tax, tax on consumption or sale of electricity, taxes on transportation of goods and services, et cetera, thus avoiding multiple layers of taxation that currently exist in India.

2. On 1 January 2015, a Cabinet resolution was passed to replace the Planning Commission with the newly formed NITI Aayog (National Institution for Transforming India). The objective was to provide proper and critical strategies and directions in which the development process can take place. One of the major initiatives of NITI Aayog was to start ranking states on various parameters. Another significant initiative of NITI Aayog is starting 'Aspirational District Program (ADP) to quickly and effectively transform the 112 most underdeveloped districts across the country. The third significant initiative of NITI Aayog is the Atal Innovation mission. AIM has two functions: Promote entrepreneurship by encouraging innovators to become entrepreneurs through financial support as well as mentorship. Promote Innovation by creating a platform where ideas are generated through like-minded individuals.

3. Connecting India: The country is upgrading its transportation networks, including a planned bullet train, new airports, and improved highways to connect the country like never before. To ease transportation and daily commute for the urban citizen, a record number of metro rail projects have been approved and commissioned across several cities. Metro connectivity is now in 20 cities in 2023 from 5 cities in 2014. 2435 electric buses are now deployed across the country. The number of operational airports almost double from 74 in 2014 to 148 in 2023.

4. Ensuring every government initiative treats all citizens as equals and no appeasement to ensure social harmony.

5. Extensive use of technology.

6. Removal of archaic laws that have been misused for harassing people and extorting bribes.

7. Determined clampdown on corruption.

8. Plugging of leakage in Government expenditure.

9. Increased efficiency and transparency in governance.

10. Generous welfare schemes.

11. Major investment in Infrastructure Projects and the power sector.

12. Upgrading the echo system significant progress has been made in the transmission sector. Since 2014, an extensive network of transmission lines spanning nearly two lakh circuit kilometers has been established connecting the entire country into one largest grid operating at a single frequency.

13. In the power sector, focus on expanding generation capacity, enhancing transmission networks, increasing access to electricity, promoting renewable energy and implementing comprehensive reforms.

14. Accelerating defence production in India. The Government is continuously working with defence industries and their associations to remove the challenges faced by them and promote defence production in the country. Several policy reforms have been taken to achieve the objective of ease of doing business, including the integration of MSMEs and startups into the supply chain. Due to these policies, the industries, including MSMEs and start-ups, are forthcoming in defence design, development and manufacturing and there is almost a 200 per cent increase in the number of defence licenses issued to the industries in the last 7-8 years by the Government. These measures have given a boost to the defence industrial manufacturing ecosystem in the country and generated tremendous employment opportunities. As a result of the consistent efforts of the Ministry of Defence, the value of defence production in the Financial Year (FY) 2022-23 has crossed the figure of Rs one lakh crore for the first time. The value currently stands at Rs 1,06,800 crore

and it will go further up. The current value of defence production in FY 2022-23 is a rise of more than 12 per cent over FY 2021-22, when the figure was Rs 95,000 crore.

15. Foreign Policy Inclusive approach with a focus on collaboration and cooperation. While there was continuity in major policies, the process had changed under PM Modi: he displayed a keenness to play an important role in shaping the international environment while managing conflicting interests in India's favor. The hesitancy witnessed earlier due to rivalry among nations and unwillingness to hurt their sentiments, has been replaced by boldness with a clear objective that relations with India are for mutual benefit and not against their rivals.

16. Bold decisions like the abolition of Article 370, Citizens Acts, and demonetization, hit back at Pakistan for its mischief's as exemplified by surgical strikes and the Balakot air strike.

17. Free food grains to 80 crore people during the pandemic which continued even after the pandemic was over

18. Country-wide validity of Ration cards.

19. Building Toilets that protect the dignity of women.

20. Electricity in every Village.

21. Affordable internet. The government has so far (July 2023) invested about $8.5 billion in the rural internet connectivity scheme that aims to provide fast broadband internet connectivity to all the six lakh villages in the country. "Today close to 850 million people have internet access. But that is not enough. We will augment it with an investment of $13 billion to make sure high quality broadband internet reaches every corner of this country," Ashwini Vaishnaw, Union IT Minister

22. Schemes to provide houses and piped drinking water to every household.

23. Anti-Terrorism Strategy PM Modi made a strategy shift vis-à-vis Pakistan after the Uri terrorist attack, advocating the elimination of terrorism from the subcontinent. He gave Full powers to authority in Kashmir to deal with terror. Modi asserted India's resolve to take

24. Strong decisions by giving a befitting reply to Pakistan sponsored terror through surgical strikes followed by the Balakot airstrike. It was the first time in the history of India that the country had adopted such an aggressive posture after a terrorist strike. Modi by destroying terror launch pads twice on foreign soil made India's intent clear to Pakistan that it won't be spared if it resorts to such terror tactics. Not just Pakistan; even a powerful neighbor like China has acknowledged the fact that this new India won't budge, and it had to make a retreat in border skirmishes. The country has felt much safer and secure during Modi's 10 years tenure.

25. Modi doesn't hesitate to fire underachievers.

26. Smart Cities: India is building 100 smart cities equipped with modern infrastructure, including high speed internet, clean energy, and efficient transportation systems.

27. Alternative Energy/ Renewable Energy: India is investing in solar energy, to generate 40% of its electricity from renewable sources by 2030. India is investing in wind, solar, and other forms of renewable energy to reduce dependence on fossil fuels and combat climate change.

28. Preserving Biodiversity: India is protecting its forests and wildlife through conservation efforts and initiatives like Project Tiger.

29. Artificial Intelligence: India is leading the way in AI research, with Indian companies developing cutting-edge technologies in fields like cloud computing and machine learning.

30. Space Exploration: India is expanding its space program,

with plans for manned missions and lunar exploration shortly.

31. Biotechnology: India is making strides in medical research, with innovative biotech companies working on new treatments for a range of diseases.

32. Education Reforms: India is expanding access to education and making sure that all its citizens have the skills they need to succeed in the modern world. The Modi government has brought a crucial turnaround in medical education. Few government colleges, high fees in private medical colleges, and massive corruption in seat allocation had severely limited opportunities for medical education. In the last nine years, the Modi government has approved/established new AIIMS in several States, and a large number of new medical colleges. These include the first-ever AIIMS in the Northeast in Assam. Further, the government's bold decision to replace the Medical Council of India with the National Medical Commission has ended corruption in medical education. In 'New India', talented students from humble backgrounds can also fulfill their dream of becoming a doctor.

33. Banking Reforms: The government introduced a series of reforms to clean up bad loans and recapitalize state owned banks. The Insolvency and Bankruptcy Code, introduced in 2016, has helped in faster resolution of stressed assets. The government's reforms have made it easier for banks to recover bad loans, which have helped inject more credit into the economy.

34. Privatization of Air India: Air India was a chronically sick and loss making Public Sector Undertaking. It cost taxpayers around $1 billion a year to keep airline's aircrafts flying. In January, 2022, Air India was privatized and Government has approved Tata Group's Rs 18,000-crore bid for the state-owned carrier, Air India. A privatized Air India will cease to be a drain on the exchequer. 34. India's quick and effective.

35. Response to the COVID-19 pandemic was supported by its roll out of the world's largest vaccination drive and those too using indigenously developed vaccines. In a landmark shift from the past, when the citizens had to wait for decades for the start of vaccination drives, PM Modi lead government ensured the administration of more than 2.2 billion doses of COVID-19 vaccine in a short span years. 35. Strategic importance of having a chip packaging plant within the country: India is entering the manufacturing fray with a $10billion incentive package for the semiconductor industry. US memory chip maker Micron Technology on 23/9/23 initiated the construction of its semiconductor packaging plant in Gujarat, India's first such facility which is expected to spur the country's chip manufacturing ambitions. Micron has selected Tata Projects to build the semiconductor assembly and test facility in Sanand town, near Ahmedabad with both signing a formal agreement during groundbreaking ceremony. Micron also said it has begun the recruitment process for the new plant. The plant is to be developed in two phases. Phase one will include a 5,00,000-squarefoot clean-room space, scheduled to be operational by late 2024.

36. India liberalized the policy governing drones operation in India via the Drones Rules 2021. A slew of positive announcements related to the segment. For example, the Cabinet's approval of INR 120 Cr PLI scheme, a ban on the import of drones – intended to boost domestic manufacturing, and the drone certification scheme to ensure safety and quality requirements are a few positive steps. Besides, the establishment of digital airspace mapping for drones alongside announcements such as Drone Shakti and Kisan Drones has been touted as a step in the right direction by experts.

37. Religious Projects: Religious tourism sites have been taken care of and developed for the first time for the ease of religious pilgrimage and revival of religious tourism. The "Pilgrimage Rejuvenation and Spiritual Augmentation

Drive (PRASAD)" scheme aims at integrating pilgrimage destinations in a prioritized, planned and sustainable manner to provide a complete religious tourism experience and it is because of this scheme that religious tourism has been revived in the country.

Strong decisions by giving a befitting reply to Pakistan sponsored terror through surgical strikes followed by the Balakot airstrike. It was the first time in the history of India that the country had adopted such an aggressive posture after a terrorist strike. Modi by destroying terror launch pads twice on foreign soil made India's intent clear to Pakistan that it won't be spared if it resorts to such terror tactics. Not just Pakistan; even a powerful neighbor like China has acknowledged the fact that this new India won't budge, and it had to make a retreat in border skirmishes. The country has felt much safer and secure during Modi's 10 years tenure.